From the First Day of School to the Last

April

Written by Rebecca Stark
Cover Illustrated by Karen Sigler
Text Illustrated by Koryn Agnello
and Karen Sigler

ISBN 1-56644-996-0

© 1998 Educational Impressions, Inc., Hawthorne, NJ

Printed in the U.S.A.

Table of Contents

To the Teacher

From the First Day of School to the Last is a series of reproducible monthly activity books to help you make every day a special day for your students. Each volume contains a wealth of critical-and-creative thinking, seasonal, creative-writing, and poetry activities that correlate with the events of the month. You'll find at least one activity for every day of the month. Also included are several mini-units and at least one literature unit. These units, too, tie in with monthly and seasonal events. A crossword puzzle provides a great culminating activity!

At the end of each book is a clip art section. Clip art may be enlarged or reduced for any non-commercial use in your classroom. The blank calendar, like the clip art, may be laminated for your convenience.

I hope these books bring enjoyment to you and your students. . .
From the First Day of School to the Last!

Rebecca Stark

(Not Just) OPENERS FOR APRIL

Use these enrichment activities at the start of class, the end of class, as homework assignments, or any time you choose!

April 1

April 1 is April Fools' Day. The custom of playing practical jokes on this date has been observed in many countries for several centuries. In France the fooled person is called a *poisson d'avril,* or April fish. In Scotland the victim is called a cuckoo. Think of an elaborate, but harmless practical joke you could play on someone. Write a paragraph describing the details of your scheme.

April 2

Danish fairy-tale writer Hans Christian Andersen, was born on April 2, 1805. Alone or with your cooperative group, create a stick-puppet skit based on one of his tales. Perform your skit for a younger audience.

7

April 3

Washington Irving was born on April 3, 1783, in New York City. He is known as the "inventor of the short story." One of his best known characters was Rip Van Winkle, a man who took a 20-year-long nap. Suppose someone in your town fell asleep twenty years ago and just woke up! Research and find out what would have changed. Write a story.

April 4

Dorothea Dix was born in Maine on April 4, 1802. Create a plaque that honors her effort to help those less fortunate than she.

April 5

Colin Powell, Chairman of the Joint Chiefs of Staff under President Bush, was born on April 5, 1937. He was the first African-American to hold this very important position. Explain what is meant by "Joint Chiefs of Staff."

April 6

The North Pole was discovered on April 6, 1909. Although Robert Peary, the leader of the expedition, is most often credited with the discovery, some believe he was not really the first to arrive at the pole. Research and find out who may have reached it first.

8

April 7

WHO was organized on this date in 1948. What is meant by WHO? What kind of word is *WHO?*

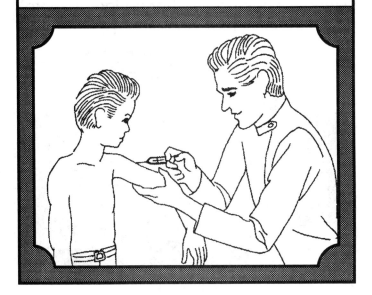

April 8

On April 8, 1974, the crowd stood and cheered as baseball great Hank Aaron rounded the bases. Why?

April 9

On April 9, 1963, Sir Winston Churchill, former prime minister of England, was made an honorary citizen of the United States. Use these clues to learn the identity of the man made an honorary citizen by many states in 1784.

CLUES

1. He was born in France on September 6, 1757.

2. He fought for the Americans and was made a major general during the American War for Independence.

3. He persuaded King Louis XVI to send an expeditionary army to assist the Americans.

April 10

Joseph Pulitzer was born on April 10, 1847, in Hungary. Explain what is meant by the Pulitzer Prizes.

9

April 11

On April 11, 1898, President McKinley made the following statement:
"In the name of humanity, in the name of civilization, in behalf of endangered American interests which give us the right and duty to speak and act, the war in Cuba must stop." Under what circumstances did he make it?

April 12

Children's author Beverly Cleary was born on April 12, 1916. Among her best known works are those about Ramona Quimby and those about Henry Huggins. Read a book from either series. Create a plot for a new book in that series.

RAMONA THE PEST BY BEVERLY CLEARY

April 13

On April 13, 1945, Harry S. Truman made this statement to reporters:
"When they told me yesterday what had happened, I felt like the moon, the stars, and all the planets had fallen on me." Explain what had happened to cause him to make that statement.

April 14

President Abraham Lincoln and his wife were enjoying a play at Ford's Theater in Washington, D.C., on April 14, 1865, when the President was fatally shot by John Wilkes Booth. Bitter about the outcome of the war, Booth shouted, *"Sic semper tyrannis!"* (This always to tyrants.) Unscramble the letters to find out what else Booth supposedly said after he shot Lincoln.

HTE TOSUH SI

VANEGED.

10

April 15

On April 15, 1947, Jackie Robinson made history by becoming the first black baseball player to play in the major leagues. Do you think this took courage? Explain your point of view.

April 16

Silent-film star Charlie Chaplin was born on April 16, 1889, in London, England. His best known character was the little tramp. Pantomime, or acting that consists mostly of gesture, is important in silent films. Alone or with your cooperative group, choose a selection from a book you have read. Pantomime an episode in that book.

April 17

Archaeologist Sir Leonard Woolley was born in London on April 7, 1880. His excavation of the ancient Sumerian city of Ur, now part of Iraq, did a lot to further our knowledge of ancient Mesopotamia. Archaeology is the systematic recovery and study of the material evidence of past human life and culture. See how many words of 3 or more letters you can form by using the letters in the word *archaeology.*

A-R-C-H-A-E-O-L-O-G-Y

April 18

On April 18, 1906, at 5:13 A.M. a severe earthquake hit San Francisco, California. Over 500 city blocks, including 28,000 buildings, were destroyed. Some estimates put the property damage as high as $500 million. About 700 people died, and about 250,000 were left homeless. Much of the damage was caused by the fire that followed the quake. San Francisco lies on the San Andreas Fault. Identify the San Andreas Fault and explain its significance.

11

April 19

On April 19, 1775, Captain John Parker made the following statement: "Stand your ground! Don't fire unless fired upon. But if they mean to have a war, let it begin here!" Answer these questions:

1. To whom did he say it?
2. During what battle did he say it?
3. What war was about to begin?
4. To whom did "they" refer?

April 20

Most consider Yellowstone National Park in Wyoming to be the first U.S. national park; however, forty years earlier, on April 20, 1832, Congress established Hot Springs, consisting of 911 acres, as a reservation. It wasn't until 1921 that it was designated Hot Springs National Park. Find out where Hot Springs is located. Explain why it is so named.

April 21

German educator Friedrich Froebel was born on April 21, 1782. He is best known as the originator and developer of kindergarten education. In his honor, prepare a lesson to teach kindergarten children about baby animals.

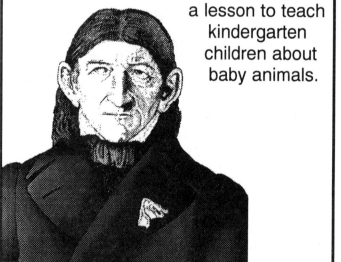

April 22

American humorist Erma Bombeck died on this date in 1996. She used the experiences of her life in the suburbs as the basis for her humorous columns and books. Create a plot in which you turn an everyday experience into a humorous story.

12

April 23

William Shakespeare was born in Stratford-on-Avon, England, on April 23, 1564. Read the following quotes. Which one is **not** attributed to William Shakespeare?

1. *All the world's a stage.*
2. *Parting is such sweet sorrow.*
3. *What's in a name? That which we call a rose By any other name would smell as sweet.*
4. *In this world nothing is certain but death and taxes.*

April 24

The Library of Congress was authorized on this date in 1800. At first housed in the Capitol, it was destroyed in 1814. In 1897 the Library of Congress moved to its permanent headquarters. Find out how the Library of Congress was destroyed.

April 25

Broadcast journalist and producer Edward R. Murrow was born on April 25, 1908, in Greensboro, North Carolina. He anchored the television series *See It Now,* which was an innovative hour-long weekly news digest. He also served as host on *Person to Person,* for which he interviewed celebrities in their homes.

Choose a famous person you would like to interview. Create five questions you would ask that person.

April 26

John Jay Audubon was born in Haiti on April 26, 1785. Find out what Audubon is known for. Create a quatrain in his honor.

13

April 27

Animator Walter Lantz was born in New Rochelle, New York, on April 27, 1900. His most famous cartoon character was Woody Woodpecker. Woody made his debut in a bit part in the 1940 cartoon short "Knock, Knock." Lantz said that the inspiration for the character was a pesky woodpecker that disturbed his honeymoon. Create a fact file about woodpeckers; include at least five facts.

April 28

James Monroe, the fifth President of the United States, was born in Virginia on April 28, 1758. In 1823 he proclaimed in his presidential message what has come to be known as the Monroe Doctrine. Its principles had been prepared in part by Monroe's secretary of state, John Quincy Adams. Write a sentence that summarizes the Monroe Doctrine.

April 29

On April 29, 1913, Gideon Sundback of New Jersey obtained a patent for "separable fasteners." Today we call his invention the "zipper." The word was at first a B.F. Goodrich trademark for boots with slide fasteners; it was named for the sound it made. In time the words "zipper" and "zip" became part of the general vocabulary. "Zipper" is an example of onomatopoeia. Explain the term and give two other examples.

April 30

Railroad engineer John Luther Jones, better known as Casey Jones, died on April 30, 1900. The ballad by T. Lawrence Siebert and Eddie Newton, published in 1909, made him a national folk hero. Find out what it was about his death that led to this myth.

April Fools' Day

The first of April, some do say,
Is set apart for All Fools' Day,
But why the people call it so
Nor I, nor they themselves, do know.

Old English Almanac

Write your own poem about April Fools' Day. It can be about the holiday itself, about a trick you have played on someone, or about a trick someone played on you.

_____

_____

_____

_____

_____

_____

Optical Illusions

Sometimes our own eyes play tricks on us! We call these deceptive images "optical illusions."

Explanation: This is an example of the type of ambiguous figure used by psychologists in their experiments in the field of visual perception. This particular one was devised by psychologist Edward Boring. He named it "My Wife and My Mother-in-Law." There are two alternative modes of perceiving it: as an attractive young girl with her head turned from the viewer and as a witch-like old lady with her head buried in her wrap. The same set of physical lines striking the retina gives rise to two distinctive perceptual images. Once both modes have been recognized, however, the perceiver can easily identify each.

What Do You See?

The gray ring appears to be uniformly bright. Place a thin line or pencil along the line where the black and white meet. Which half of the gray ring appears darker? Why?

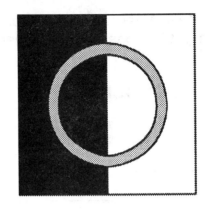

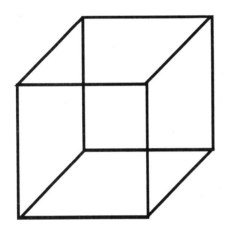

This is called the Necker Cube. Does it project up or down? The answer depends partly upon where you focus your vision.

Look at this reversible staircase. Shifting the focus of your visual perception can reverse the way the stairs seem to go.

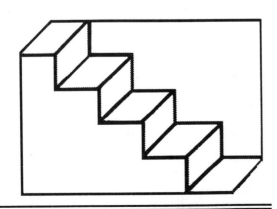

How many cubes do you see?

Keep America Beautiful

April is Keep America Beautiful Month. Think about the public areas of your town or city. What might be done to beautify them? List your ideas below.

SCHOOL GROUNDS

_____

_____

_____

_____

_____

_____

_____

_____

_____

DOWNTOWN / SHOPPING AREAS

_____

_____

_____

_____

_____

_____

_____

_____

_____

RECREATION FIELDS

_____

_____

_____

_____

_____

_____

_____

_____

_____

RESIDENTIAL AREAS

_____

_____

_____

_____

_____

_____

_____

_____

_____

That's Better!

Choose one of the areas listed on the previous page. Write a brief paragraph explaining what changes might be made in order to beautify the area.

_____

_____

_____

_____

_____

_____

Now draw a picture of what the area will look like after all the improvements have been made.

International Children's Book Day

April 2 has been designated International Children's Book Day. On this date in 1805 Hans Christian Andersen was born in Odense, Denmark. His fairy tales are among the most popular in the world. Unlike the villains in many other folk tales, Andersen's villains are human weaknesses, such as selfishness or vanity, rather than witches and ogres.

List at least three fairy tales written by Hans Christian Andersen.

Choose one of the fairy tales you listed. Create your own illustrated version of it.

Read a book by an author whose work you have never read. Tell why you would or would not recommend it to others. Would you want to read other works by this author?

Who is your favorite author? Write a letter to that author. Explain why you enjoy his or her work.

See Children's Book Week in the *November* volume of this series for additional activities.

Jane Goodall

Animal behaviorist Jane Goodall was born on April 3, 1934, in London, England. She is best known for her studies of chimpanzees in the wild. For many years Ms. Goodall observed the chimpanzees in their natural habitat and kept detailed notes of what she observed. Among the new information she discovered was the fact that although chimpanzees are basically vegetarian, they also will hunt, kill, and eat small game. Another interesting fact she learned was that these animals fashion simple tools.

CHIMPANZEES

Chimpanzees belong to the order of mammals called Primates. There are two main groups of Primates: prosimians, or lower primates, and anthropoids, or higher primates. Like humans, chimpanzees and other great apes are higher primates.

CHARACTERISTICS OF PRIMATES

First Toe and First Thumb
    One or both are opposable, or able to be placed opposite something else.

Eyes on Front of Face

Relatively Large Brain

Nails, Not Claws, on Most Fingers and Toes

18 to 36 Teeth, Which Are Not Highly Specialized

Omnivorous Diet

Large Variety in Weight and Size

Primates

Unscramble these letters to spell the name of species of primates.

M U H N A   __ __ __ __ __ (1)

O A B B O N   __ __ __ __ __ __ (4)

K O M N Y E   __ __ __ __ __ __ (1)

R O G I A L L   __ __ __ __ __ __ __ (2)

A T R S R I E*   __ __ __ __ __ __ __ (4)

D R M A N I L L   __ __ __ __ __ __ __ __ (2)

N I H C M P A E E Z   __ __ __ __ __ __ __ __ __ __ (5)

N I G B B O   __ __ __ __ __ __ (2)

E L M R U*   __ __ __ __ __ (2)

G R O A N T U A N   __ __ __ __ __ __ __ __ __ (4)

T E S O M R A M   __ __ __ __ __ __ __ __ (6)

For each unscrambled word, count the number of spaces as indicated by the number in parentheses. Write down the letter above that space. The letters will spell the name of the species to which modern humans belong.

Modern humans belong to the species

__ __ __ __   __ __ __ __ __ __ __.

*Those followed by an (*) are lower primates. The others are higher primates.

Make a diorama showing the environment of a chimpanzee in the wild.

Plan a birthday party for a chimp. What foods will you serve?

Choose a higher primate other than humans. Compare and contrast that animal and humans. In other words, tell how they are alike and how they are different.

Once widespread throughout the equatorial region of Africa, the chimpanzee population has been greatly reduced. Figures in 1992 showed only three countries with chimp populations above 10,000: Zaire, Gabon, and Côte d'Ivoire. Locate these places on a map.

Studies have shown that chimpanzees and gorillas are capable of comprehending and using language. Read *Koko's Kitten* and/or *Koko's Story,* by Dr. Francine Patterson. Write a sentence explaining who Koko is.

Dian Fossey, like Jane Goodall, lived in the wild in order to learn about the daily life of the great apes. Research her work. In your opinion, what was her greatest contribution?

23

Daylight-Savings Time

In 1884 an international system of time zones was adopted. The zones are based upon the lines of longitude that we use to divide the surface of the Earth. There are twenty-four zones in all. Within each of those zones, time is the same.

Daylight-savings time is observed throughout most of the United States. Every year, on the first Sunday in April at 2:00 A.M., clocks are set ahead an hour. The clocks are once again set back to standard time at 2:00 A.M. on the last Sunday in October.

Sometimes it is hard to remember which way to turn the clocks. The following will help you remember whether to set your clocks ahead an hour or back an hour:

← SPRING FORWARD. →
FALL BEHIND.

Create a cartoon that shows whether you lose or gain an hour of sleep when you set the clock ahead in April.

Many countries adopted daylight-savings time during World War I. During World War II, the United States went to daylight-savings time from February 9, 1942, through September 30, 1945. See if you can find out why.

24

Longitude and Time Zones

If you look at a globe, you will notice that there are lines running from pole to pole. Called lines of longitude, or meridians, each of these lines is given a number of degrees. The symbol for degrees is a small, raised circle (°).

On a globe, lines of longitude are shown in intervals, or spaces, of fifteen degrees: 0°, 15°, 30°, and so on, to 180°. The zero degree line, which is called the prime meridian, runs through Greenwich, England. Longitude lines east of the prime meridian are east longitude lines. Those west of the prime meridian are west longitude lines. East and west lines meet at the 180° line, or 180th meridian. This line is halfway around the world from the prime meridian.

We divide the Earth into time zones. Each time zone includes about fifteen degrees of longitude. That's because as the Earth rotates, it moves through 15 degrees of longitude every hour. There are twenty-four time zones in all. One for each hour of the day.

There are four time zones in the continental United States. Going from east to west, they are as follows: Eastern Time, Central Time, Mountain Time, and Pacific Time. Alaska is in the Alaskan Time Zone. Hawaii is in the Hawaii-Aleutian Time Zone.

TIME ZONES OF THE UNITED STATES

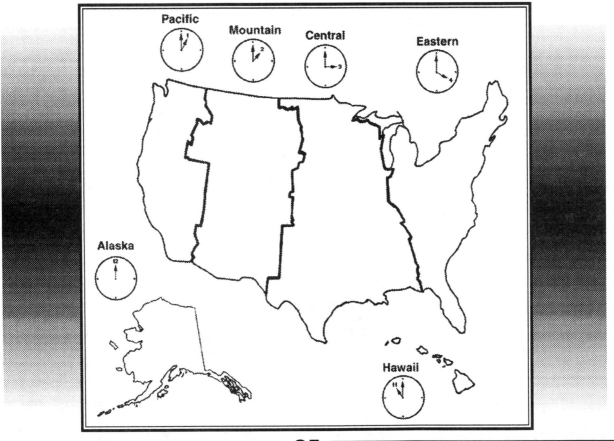

Find out in which time zones the following places are located: Chicago, Illinois; Miami, Florida; Salt Lake City, Utah; and Las Vegas, Nevada.

Look at the time zones on the map. Why, do you think, do they zigzag?

Suppose it is midnight in New York City. Name a city where it is 11:00 P.M.

If it is 9 o'clock in the morning in New York City, what time is it in Los Angeles, California?

Obtain a globe. Locate the following: prime meridian; Greenwich, England; the International Date Line; and the time zone in which you live.

Find out what is meant by the International Date Line. If it is January 3 east of the line, what is the date west of the line?

Booker T. Washington

African-American educator Booker T. Washington was born on April 5, 1856, in Franklin County, Virginia. The facts listed below are out of order. Use context clues to put them in the proper sequence.

___ Booker had to leave the school in Malden to work in the coal mines; he also worked for Mrs. Ruffner, the mine owner's wife.

___ In 1881 Booker T. Washington was appointed the first president of the Tuskegee Normal and Industrial Institute.

___ On Booker's first day of school in Malden, his teacher asked his last name.

___ In 1865, after the Civil War ended, Booker's family moved to Malden, West Virginia.

___ Fortunately, Mrs. Ruffner allowed Booker to attend school part of the time.

___ There was no school when Booker first moved to Malden. When one opened, his stepfather said he could attend if he promised to continue to work before and after school.

___ He didn't have a last name; he chose the name Washington.

___ Booker worked his way through Hampton and was graduated in 1875.

___ After graduating from Hampton, Booker returned to Malden to teach school.

___ When Booker was sixteen, he left the coal mines and the Ruffners; he headed for Hampton Institute, a school for blacks.

___ On January 1, 1863, the Emancipation Proclamation, issued by President Lincoln, freed all the slaves in the rebel states. Booker and his family were no longer slaves.

What Does the "T" Stand For?

Use the clues to fill in the answers. The letters in the boxes will spell Booker T. Washington's middle name.

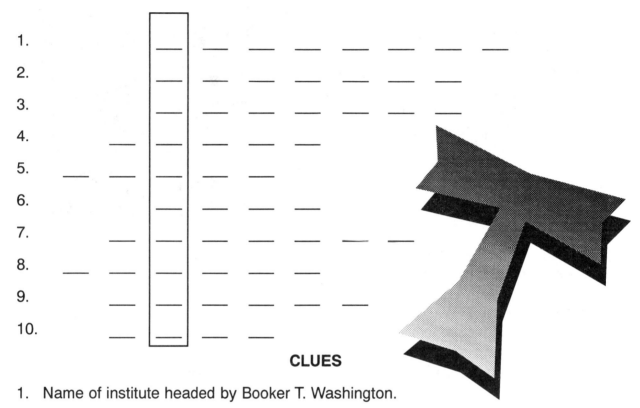

1. ____ ___ ___ ___ ___ ___ ___ ___
2. ___ ___ ___ ___ ___ ___
3. ___ ___ ___ ___ ___
4. ___ ___ ___ ___ ___
5. ___ ___ ___ ___ ___ ___
6. ___ ___ ___ ___ ___
7. ___ ___ ___ ___ ___
8. ___ ___ ___ ___ ___
9. ___ ___ ___ ___ ___ ___
10. ___ ___ ___ ___

CLUES

1. Name of institute headed by Booker T. Washington.

2. State in which number 1 is located.

3. President who issued the Emancipation Proclamation.

4. Type of war being fought when Booker was a child.

5. Booker was born one.

6. Booker's family became this when the Emancipation Proclamation was issued.

7. Booker's profession as an adult.

8. Adjective used to describe a school to train teachers.

9. These are taught at an industrial school.

10. Type of mine Booker worked in.

The "T" stands for the name _____.

Booker T. Washington wrote a book entitled *Up from Slavery*. Find out what kind of book this is.

Research George Washington Carver. Explain his relationship with Booker T. Washington.

Research W.E.B. Du Bois. As Du Bois, write a letter to a friend explaining why you disagree with Booker T. Washington's philosophy.

Booker T. Washington was an important black leader. Many whites at the time believed he spoke for *all* blacks. Do you think that one person can speak for *all* members of an ethnic or religious group? Explain.

A Safety Pin

The safety pin was invented by Walter Hunt of New York City. He obtained the patent for the invention on April 10, 1849. It took him only three hours to conceive the idea, make the model, and obtain the patent. He immediately sold these patent rights for one hundred dollars.

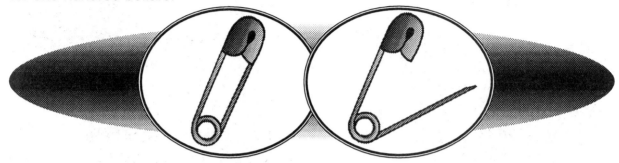

Brainstorm and think of all the possible things you can do with safety pins. Try to think of some creative, unusual uses!

_____ _____
_____ _____
_____ _____
_____ _____
_____ _____
_____ _____
_____ _____

Draw a picture of your most creative idea!

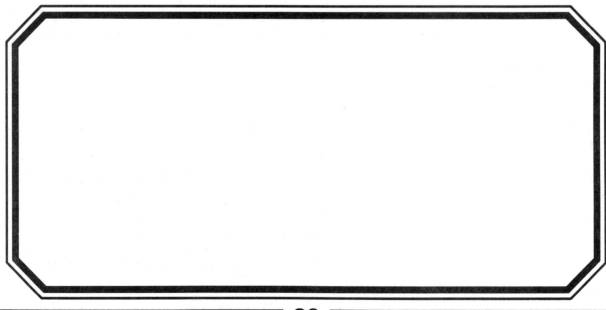

Be Kind to Animals

The American Society for the Prevention of Cruelty to Animals was incorporated on April 10, 1866. The ASPCA, as it is known, encourages the proper care and treatment of animals.

Pets have basic rights. Create a Bill of Rights for pets.

Read *Shiloh*, by Phyllis Reynolds Naylor. It is about a boy who rescues a dog being mistreated by its owner. Write a review of the book.

Suppose you witnessed the abuse of a pet. What would you do? Create a plan of action. Write a paragraph describing your plan.

Write a letter to your local chapter of the ASPCA. Ask for a copy of their goals.

Millions of animals are used each year in laboratory experimentation. Cosmetics, shampoos, and food additives are often tested on animals before they are given to animals. Medicines are usually tried on animals before they are given to human subjects. Some people believe this testing is cruel. Others believe it is necessary in order to protect humans. Choose a point of view and write a letter to the editor of your local newspaper.

Dear Editor:

_____

_____

_____

_____

_____

_____

The Space Shuttle

On April 12, 1981, the *Columbia,* the first American space shuttle, lifted off for the first time from the Kennedy Space Center at Cape Canaveral, Florida. Astronauts John Young and Robert Crippen were in the cockpit. The main objective of the mission was to show that the vehicle was capable and reliable enough to deliver people and materials into space and then return them to Earth. There would be only one chance to land safely! Happily, they did just that!

The shuttle uses its three engines and two rocket boosters to lift off like a rocket. Find out how it lands.

If given the opportunity, would you like to ride in a space shuttle? Write a letter to NASA accepting or rejecting their invitation to ride on one.

Find out what made the space shuttle different from previous spacecraft.

On January 28, 1986, the space shuttle *Challenger* exploded 74 seconds after its take-off. All seven crew members were killed. Also killed was teacher Christa McAuliffe, the first ordinary citizen in space. Do you think the men and women who participate in the space program are heroes and heroines? Explain your point of view in a brief paragraph.

Thomas Jefferson

Thomas Jefferson was born on April 13, 1743. He grew up in Albemarle County in the western part of Virginia. Thomas was very bright and had many **varied** interests.

When Thomas was sixteen, he entered the College of William and Mary in Williamsburg. After completing his studies there, he studied law and eventually gained a **reputation** as a fine lawyer. Like most well-educated landowners of the time, he decided to enter politics. In 1768 he was elected to the Virginia legislature, which was called the House of Burgesses.

At about this time Thomas set his mind on a more personal project. He had read many books on **architecture** and was about to put his knowledge to good use. Thomas planned and **supervised** the building of his new **mansion,** which he named Monticello. It was only partially built when he moved into Monticello in 1770. The beautiful home was complete, however, when Thomas and his bride, Martha Wayles Skelton, married on January 1, 1772.

Life in the colonies was uncertain. Talk of revolution had spread. In 1773 Thomas Jefferson helped organize a Committee of Correspondence in Virginia. This and other committees were set up to help the colonies unite against Britain.

The next year the First Continental Congress met. Although Jefferson was unable to attend, he sent a paper describing his views. That paper, read at the meeting, argued that the British Parliament had no control over the American colonies. In the spring of 1775, when the Second Continental Congress met, Jefferson expressed his own views.

On July 4, 1776, the **document** known as the Declaration of Independence was adopted. It had been **drafted** by Thomas Jefferson. Few changes had been made in it; however, there was one important **exception.** The section in which Jefferson had **denounced** slavery was not included.

In September 1776 Thomas Jefferson **resigned** from Congress and returned to the Virginia House of Delegates. He headed a committee to **revise** Virginia's laws. Jefferson was responsible for many important **reforms,** including the separation of church and state.

In 1779 the Virginia Assembly elected Thomas Jefferson the second governor of the state; he served for two terms. His inability to stop the British invasion of Virginia led to an **investigation** of his actions. The results of that investigation brought him nothing but praise. He was even chosen as a **delegate** to the Continental Congress; nevertheless, Jefferson was deeply hurt by the investigation. He resigned from Congress and said he would never again hold public office.

Jefferson returned to Monticello and enjoyed his life there—until Martha died in September 1782. At first he was very **depressed,** but gradually, he began to get on with his life. When Congress asked him to join John Adams and Benjamin Franklin in France in May 1784 to negotiate treaties of commerce, he accepted. When Franklin resigned as **Minister** to France in 1785, Jefferson replaced him.

In October 1789 Jefferson returned to America. A letter from the newly elected President Washington awaited him. It asked him to be the nation's first secretary of state. Thomas Jefferson **reluctantly** agreed. He remained in that position until December 31, 1793, determined to get Monticello back in order. He never expected to return to public office.

Jefferson was mistaken. When Washington announced that he would not run for a third term, Jefferson became a candidate without even expressing an interest! Others did all his campaigning. John Adams, who received the most votes, won. Jefferson, with the second highest number of votes, became vice president. Adams was a Federalist. Jefferson was a Republican.

In 1800 Thomas Jefferson actively campaigned against John Adams. This time Jefferson won. He would serve two terms.

The most important event of Jefferson's presidency was the purchase of the Louisiana Territory from France in 1803. It doubled the size of the United States. Jefferson asked Meriwether Lewis and William Clark to head an **expedition** to explore the area. They brought back valuable information.

One of Thomas Jefferson's proudest achievements came late in his life: the creation of the University of Virginia. It was built in Charlottesville, near Monticello. Jefferson planned the curriculum, hired the faculty, and selected many of the library books.

Thomas Jefferson died on July 4, 1826. He had left instructions for the **inscription** on his tombstone. It read, "Here was buried Thomas Jefferson, author of the Declaration of Independence, of the **Statute** of Virginia for Religious Freedom, and Father of the University of Virginia."

NOTE: This reading selection was based on the book *Thomas Jefferson,* written by Linda Wade and published by January Productions, Inc., Hawthorne, New Jersey.

Vocabulary Match-up

The vocabulary words on the left were taken from the reading selection about Thomas Jefferson. For each word, find the appropriate meaning on the right. Look for the words in the reading selection and use context clues to help you. (These words are printed in bold in the selection.)

___ 1. reputation   A. a written or printed paper with information about something

___ 2. architecture   B. a detailed inquiry; a close examination

___ 3. supervised   C. a case where a rule does not apply

___ 4. mansion   D. a person sent with power to act for another; a representative

___ 5. document   E. characteristic or trait ascribed to a person

___ 6. drafted   F. gave up a position; quit

___ 7. exception   G. the courses of study offered by a school

___ 8. denounced   H. art and science of designing and erecting buildings

___ 9. resigned   I. improvements; changes for the better

___ 10. revise   J. with some unwillingness or resistance

___ 11. reforms   K. directed the performance of

___ 12. investigation   L. something written, engraved, or printed as a lasting record

___ 13. delegate   M. the teachers in a school

___ 14. depressed   N. a large, stately house

___ 15. reluctantly   O. a trip undertaken for a specific purpose

___ 16. expedition   P. a law enacted by a legislature

___ 17. curriculum   Q. low in spirits

___ 18. faculty   R. to change or modify

___ 19. inscription   S. condemned as evil

___ 20. statute   T. prepared; composed

Research and report on Colonial Williamsburg.

Unscramble these letters. They will spell the name of the first governor of Virginia.

A P T I R K C
E H N Y R

As secretary of state, Thomas Jefferson had many disagreements with Alexander Hamilton, secretary of the treasury. Summarize their differences.

In 1804, when Jefferson ran for his second term as President, a major change had been made in the election law. Explain.

Jefferson left instructions for the inscription on his tombstone. It summarized what he believed to be the greatest achievements of his life. Choose someone—living or dead—whom you admire. Write an inscription for that person's tombstone.

Pan-American Day

April 14 is Pan-American Day. On this date in 1890 the International Bureau of American Republics was established. The name was later changed to the Pan-American Union. Today the organization is known as the Organization of American States, or OAS. Its charter was signed on April 30, 1948, at the end of the Ninth Pan-American Conference, which was held in Bogotá, Colombia.

One of the main goals of the OAS was to prevent the spread of communism. Find out what country was expelled in 1962. Locate that country on a map.

The founding members of the OAS accepted the main principles of the Monroe Doctrine. Explain.

Create a word search of Pan-American states in the grid below.
(You may use the matching exercise on the next page as a reference.)

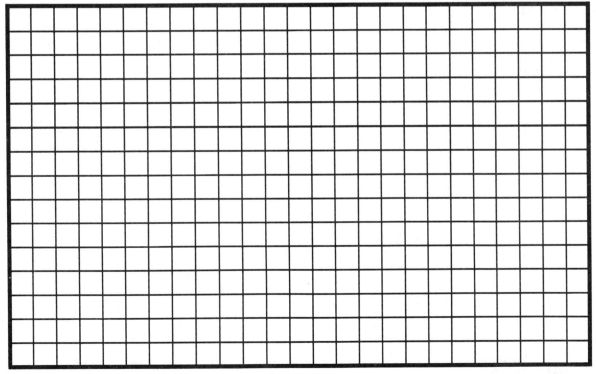

Name That Capital!

When the OAS was founded there were twenty-three members. In 1989, when Canada joined, there were thirty-three. Match each nation on the left with its capital on the right. You may use your dictionary, your encyclopedia, or another reference source.

_____ 1. Argentina	A. Santiago
_____ 2. Bolivia	B. Ottawa
_____ 3. Brazil	C. San Salvador
_____ 4. Canada	D. Tegucigalpa
_____ 5. Chile	E. Panama City
_____ 6. Colombia	F. Buenos Aires
_____ 7. Costa Rica	G. Lima
_____ 8. Dominican Republic	H. San José
_____ 9. Ecuador	I. Mexico City
_____ 10. El Salvador	J. Bogotá
_____ 11. Guatemala	K. La Paz
_____ 12. Haiti	L. Asunción
_____ 13. Honduras	M. Santo Domingo
_____ 14. Mexico	N. Guatemala City
_____ 15. Nicaragua	O. Quito
_____ 16. Panama	P. Montevideo
_____ 17. Paraguay	Q. Brasilia
_____ 18. Peru	R. Caracas
_____ 19. Uruguay	S. Port-au-Prince
_____ 20. Venezuela	T. Managua

An American Dictionary

An American Dictionary of the English Language, Noah Webster's masterpiece, was first published on April 14, 1828. At the time, it was quite controversial. Many criticized Webster for his preference for American spellings and usage rather than British. Some also found fault with his inclusion of non-literary words. Webster countered these criticisms by saying that spelling, grammar, and usage should be based on the living, spoken language. Future generations would agree with him!

Noah Webster is best known for two works. One was An American Dictionary of the English Language. Find out the name of the other work. (This work has been in print since 1783!)

At first Noah Webster planned to call his work A Dictionary of the American Language. He decided to change it to An American Dictionary of the English Language. Judge this decision.

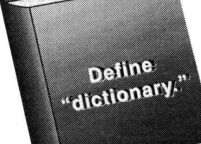

Define "dictionary."

"Dictionary order" is usually alphabetical. Brainstorm and think of other ways the words might be organized.

A dictionary may include a complete inventory of words or only a small part of it. A short list of words at the back of a book is a glossary. Create a glossary for a book about spring.

List as many different kinds of reference books as you can. Use your list to create a scrambled-word game.

Use the list you created for your scrambled-word game to create a matching game.

Create a new word game. What are the rules?

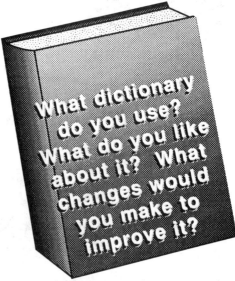

What dictionary do you use? What do you like about it? What changes would you make to improve it?

It's in the D-I-C-T-I-O-N-A-R-Y

Using only the letters found in the word "dictionary," spell out a word for each definition. The first has been done for you.

1. Used to make a word or group of words negative. **not**

2. Town of significant size and importance. _____

3. A unit of weight equal to 2,240 pounds or 1,016 kilograms. _____

4. To talk loudly and wildly. _____

5. To smooth or press clothes. _____

6. A connected line of railroad cars. _____

7. To fall as drops of water from clouds. _____

8. To draw off or flow off gradually or completely. _____

9. A public violence, disturbance, or disorder. _____

10. A tract of ground open to the sky and next to a building. _____

Add five definitions of your own. Be sure that all the letters in your answer are found in the word "dictionary" the appropriate number of times.

11. _____. _____

12. _____. _____

13. _____. _____

14. _____. _____

15. _____. _____

Exchange with classmates to solve.

Rhyme-Time Definitions

For each definition on the left, try to think of a pair of rhyming words that fits the description.

EXAMPLE: a stuffed male animal = a full bull

1. an angry parent   = a(n) _ ☐ _   _ _ _

2. a primate's shoulder garment = a(n) _ ☐ _   _ _ _ _

3. an envious ruler   = a(n) _ ☐ _ _ _   _ _ _ _

4. a particular window dressing = a(n) _ _ _ _ _ ☐ _   _ _ _ _ _ _ _

5. a fortunate bird   = a(n) ☐ _ _ _ _   _ _ _ _

6. a phony reptile   = a(n) _ _ _ _ _ ☐ _ _ _ _

7. a fast fowl   = a(n) _ _ _ _ _   _ ☐ _ _ _

8. a little amphibian that eats too much = a(n) _ _ _ _ _   _ _ ☐ _ _ _

9. a soaked puppy   = a(n) ☐ _ _   _ _ _ _

10. a cowardly lad   = a(n) _ ☐ _ _   _ _ _ _ _ _

11. a chubby rodent   = a(n) _ _ _   ☐ _ _

Now write the letters in the blocks. They will spell something that helps the flowers grow in May in the Northern Hemisphere.

_ _ _ _ _ _   _ _ _ _ _ _ _

Create your own Rhyme-Time Definitions. Exchange with classmates to solve.

1.

2.

3.

National Library Week

National Library Week begins the third Sunday in April.

The first town-supported free public library in America was established in Peterborough, New Hampshire, on April 9, 1933. Find out when your local library was established.

List the different kinds of resources that are available to you in your local library. Use it to create a brochure encouraging the residents of your town to take advantage of their public library.

In many libraries the librarian is called a media specialist. Evaluate this title. Can you think of any other appropriate titles?

Choose one of these topics: trees, insects, or birds. Prepare an annotated bibliography of books you would use to write a report on that topic. An annotated bibliography is one that adds a commentary about each book.

Interview the media specialist in your school or local library. Think of at least five questions to ask.

Find It!: A Research Activity

Students will use the resources of the school and/or local public library in order to complete this research activity.

VARIATIONS:
If your library is well stacked, you might want to conduct this activity as a contest. Divide the class into small, cooperative-learning groups. The first group to complete all twenty research items wins the contest.

Assign all twenty items to be done individually or in small, cooperative-learning groups.

Randomly assign students one or more items.

Allow students to complete the activity for extra credit.

DIRECTIONS:
For each item, students must include the following information:
> Answer to the question (if applicable)
> Book Information (This information must be included even if the student would be able to answer the question without looking it up.)
> > Title
> > Author or editor
> > Publisher
> > Page number where information was found (if applicable)

NOTE: It is best to exclude or limit the use of encyclopedias for this activity.

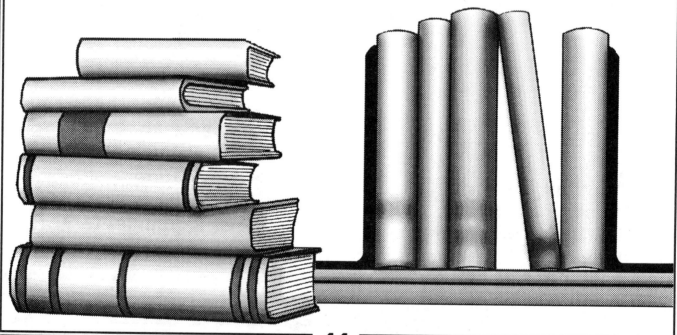

FIND IT! RESEARCH ITEMS

Remember to include the answer to the question (if applicable); the title, author (or editor), and publisher of the book; and the page number where the information was found (if applicable).

1. Charlemagne was born on April 2, c. 742. Locate a book about the Middle Ages.

_____

_____

_____

2. On April 4, 1614, John Rolfe and Pocahontas were married. Locate a fiction or non-fiction book with information about Pocahontas.

_____

_____

_____

3. What great civil rights leader was assassinated on April 4, 1968?

_____

_____

_____

4. The Olympic games were revived on April 6, 1896, after a 15-century lapse. Find a book with information about the Olympic games—ancient or modern.

_____

_____

_____

5. One of the bloodiest battles of the American Civil War took place on April 6 and 7, 1862. What was that battle?

_____

_____

_____

6. Olympic gold medalist Sonja Henie was born on April 8, 1912. Find a book about ice skating.

_____

_____

_____

7. What famous surrender took place on April 9, 1865, to basically end the American Civil War?

_____

_____

_____

8. The first Arbor Day was observed on April 10, 1872. Locate a book about trees.

_____

_____

_____

9. Clara Barton, founder of the American Red Cross, died on April 12, 1912. Find a book about nurses or other health-care workers.

_____

_____

_____

10. Tiger Woods became the youngest player ever to win the Masters golf tournament on April 11, 1997. Find a book about golf.

_____

_____

_____

11. On April 14, 1912, the cruise ship *Titanic* struck an iceberg; it sank a few hours later. Locate a book about this or another sea or air disaster.

_____

_____

_____

12. Kareen Abdul Jabbar was born on April 16, 1947. Find a book about the sport for which he is known.

_____

_____

_____

13. Wilbur Wright was born in Indiana on April 16, 1867. For what are he and his brother best known? What was his brother's name?

_____

_____

_____

14. April 16 is Holocaust Memorial Day. Find a fiction book about the Holocaust.

_____

_____

_____

15. On April 18, 1775, Paul Revere rode to warn the Minutemen that the British were coming. Which 19th-century poet wrote about "Paul Revere's Ride"?

_____

_____

_____

16. The Spanish queen who sponsored the expeditions of Christopher Columbus was born on April 22, 1451. Who was she?

_____

_____

_____

17. Sergei Sergeevich Prokofiev, composer of *Peter and the Wolf* and many other great musical works, was born in Russia on April 23, 1891. Find a book about one or more great composers.

_____

_____

_____

18. Famed jazz vocalist Ella Fitzgerald was born on April 25, 1918. Locate a book with information about jazz or jazz musicians.

_____

_____

_____

19. Ludwig Bemelmans was born on April 27, 1898. What is the name of the main character in his famous series of books?

_____

_____

_____

20. Hirohito was born on April 29, 1901. He was emperor of Japan from December 25, 1926, until he died on January 7, 1989. Find a book about Japan—ancient or modern.

_____

_____

_____

Holocaust Memorial Day

Holocaust Memorial Day is observed on April 16 to commemorate the anniversary of the Warsaw Ghetto uprising. The Nazis had confined the Jews of Warsaw to an overcrowded section known as the Warsaw Ghetto. By spring of 1943 about 400,000 Jews had been removed to the concentration camps. The 60,000 or so who remained rebelled against their oppressors. On May 16—after a month of fighting—the revolt was suppressed by the Nazis.

In what country is Warsaw located? Find it on a map.

It can be very upsetting to learn about the atrocities inflicted by the Nazis. Do you think it is important to learn about them anyway? Write a letter to the president of your school board expressing your opinion.

What can we do to prevent another Holocaust?

The people who died at the hands of the Nazis are sometimes called martyrs. Define the term "martyr."

Read a book about the Holocaust. A few suggestions are *Number the Stars*, by Lois Lowry, *Diary of a Young Girl*, by Anne Frank, and *The Devil's Arithmetic*, by Jane Yolen.

A Literature Unit

Ben and Me

by Robert Lawson

Benjamin Franklin was born on January 17, 1706, in Boston, Massachusetts.* He died on April 17, 1790. In his memory read *Ben and Me,* an unusual biography by Robert Lawson. It is written from a mouse's point of view!

*Additional activities on Benjamin Franklin are in the *January* volume of this series.

FOREWORD and Chapter I: *I, Amos*

Vocabulary: Match the vocabulary word on the left with the definition on the right.

_____ 1. altering	a.	an act intended to deceive
_____ 2. minute	b.	mourned; grieved for
_____ 3. decipher	c.	harshness; extreme intensity
_____ 4. hoax	d.	a current of air in an enclosed area (variant spelling)
_____ 5. intimacy	e.	exceptionally small
_____ 6. lamented	f.	condition of being marked by close friendship
_____ 7. vestry	g.	cold and cutting; gloomy and somber
_____ 8. severity	h.	to interpret something unclear
_____ 9. delirious	i.	room in church where sacred furnishings are kept
_____ 10. draught	j.	suffering from temporary mental confusion
_____ 11. bleak	k.	changing; making different

Comprehension & Discussion Questions

1. Why was the room and everything in it tiny?

_____

2. According to the narrator, who was responsible, at least in part, for Ben Franklin's many successes?

_____

3. What was Amos's family forced to eat when their supply of food ran out?

_____

4. Why did Amos leave home?

_____

5. Where did Amos make his new home?

_____

Follow-up Activities

1. Create an ABC's of boys' and girls' names.
2. Amos is a rodent. What distinguishing feature do rodents have? List three other rodents.

Chapters II and III: *We Invent the Franklin Stove* and *The Bargain*

Vocabulary: Match the vocabulary word on the left with the definition on the right.

_____ 1. ember	a. metal supports for holding up logs in a fireplace
_____ 2. flatiron	b. food that sustains life; sustenance
_____ 3. andirons	c. dramatic actions or gestures
_____ 4. flourishes	d. residence
_____ 5. maxim	e. braved the dangers of
_____ 6. domicile	f. a small piece of live coal or wood in a dying fire
_____ 7. hindrance	g. removing; taking off
_____ 8. subsistence	h. impediment; something that gets in the way of
_____ 9. succor	i. a heated device used for pressing clothes
_____ 10. ventured	j. stormy
_____ 11. inclement	k. a saying; a general rule of conduct
_____ 12. doffing	l. assistance in time of distress; relief

Comprehension & Discussion Questions

1. What gave Amos the idea that led to the invention of the Franklin stove?

_____

2. What did Amos suggest to protect the flour from the heat? Where did he get the idea?

_____

3. Why did Amos ask Ben if he was going to pass through the pantry?

_____

4. What did Ben say that made Amos feel good about his suggestions about the stove?

_____

5. Summarize the agreement between Amos and Ben Franklin.

_____

Follow-up Activities

1. Create an agreement between you and your pet (or a pet you would like to have) so that each benefits from the relationship.

Chapters IV and V:
Swimming and *We Do Some Printing*

Vocabulary: Match the vocabulary word on the left with the definition on the right.

____ 1. indulging	a. proceeded clumsily
____ 2. barbarous	b. depression or discouragement from loss of hope
____ 3. secluded	c. unkempt; untidy
____ 4. disported	d. yielding to; gratifying
____ 5. mongrel	e. committed; accomplished
____ 6. floundered	f. of mixed breed
____ 7. antics	g. pranks; ludicrous acts or gestures
____ 8. despondency	h. act of spreading or scattering
____ 9. disheveled	i. uncivilized; lacking refinement
____ 10. dissemination	j. resentful; jealous
____ 11. perpetrated	k. set apart from others
____ 12. envious	l. played; occupied oneself with amusements

Comprehension & Discussion Questions

1. How did Amos avoid the dog?

_____

2. Guess why Ben cried wildly when he saw the dog with his cap?

_____

3. Why did the two "country yokels" believe Ben Franklin had died?

_____

4. What pen name did Ben Franklin use in the writing of the almanacs?

_____

5. Why did Amos hide under a pile of litter for two days?

_____

Follow-up Activities

1. In Chapter IV Ben found himself in an embarrassing situation. Write about a situation that embarrassed you when it happened but that you can laugh about now.
2. Think about the adage "Haste makes waste." Relate the adage to a personal experience.

Chapters VI and VII:
Electricity and *The Lightning Rod*

Vocabulary: Match the vocabulary word on the left with the definition on the right.

____ 1. lenient	a. preoccupied excessively
____ 2. harness	b. mocked; taunted
____ 3. bidding	c. to correct; to set right
____ 4. dampen	d. merciful; not harsh
____ 5. cumbered	e. demonstration of the existence of something
____ 6. obsessed	f. quality of having a moderate estimation of one's talents, etc.
____ 7. rectify	g. to bring under control and direct the force of
____ 8. manifestation	h. deadened (a sound)
____ 9. muffled	i. cluttered up
____ 10. consoled	j. command; a demand that something be done
____ 11. jeered	k. comforted
____ 12. modesty	l. to deaden; to depress

Comprehension & Discussion Questions

1. What happened when Ben rubbed a tube with silk or fur and then touched Amos's tail with the tube? Why?

_____

2. Name the group organized by Ben to discuss electricity and other scientific ideas.

_____

3. Why were so many important people gathered in the hall?

_____

4. Why did Amos make changes in Ben's apparatus? What were the results?

_____

5. What question regarding lightning did Ben want to answer?

_____

Follow-up Activities

1. Create a chart about conductors and insulators to explain why Amos was protected by the jar.
2. Amos used sarcasm when responding to Ben's statement that his glasses had been knocked off. Define sarcasm and find the example.
3. Amos pretended to be interested in Ben's experiments. Did you ever pretend to be interested in something in order to make someone feel good? Explain.

Chapters VIII and IX:
The Kite and *War*

Vocabulary: Match the vocabulary word on the left with the definition on the right.

____ 1. deceit	a. not having normal strength
____ 2. rift	b. shook violently
____ 3. brooding	c. sudden disasters; complete failures
____ 4. treacherous	d. a break in friendly relations
____ 5. contrived	e. one who favors rapid, sweeping changes
____ 6. frail	f. an attempt to mislead
____ 7. incessant	g. an agitator
____ 8. convulsed	h. thinking long and anxiously about something
____ 9. catastrophes	i. distinguished; eminent
____ 10. radical	j. not to be trusted; traitorous
____ 11. firebrand	k. not stopping or letting up
____ 12. prominent	l. invented; made in a skillful way

Comprehension & Discussion Questions

1. What "act of deceit" caused a rift in Ben and Amos's friendship?

_____

2. What did Ben finally do to win back Amos's friendship?

_____

3. Why did Ben sail for England? Why didn't Amos accompany him?

_____

4. Who was Red?

_____

5. According to Amos, upon what document was the Declaration of Independence based?

_____

Follow-up Activities

1. The author used personification when about to describe how Ben tricked Amos: "That Deceit could raise its ugly head in such idyllic surroundings…seems particularly painful." Define personification. Write an original sentence using personification.
2. As Amos, write a letter to Benjamin Franklin expressing your feelings regarding the kite incident.

Chapters X and XI:
La Belle France and *At Court*

Vocabulary: Match the vocabulary word on the left with the definition on the right.

_____ 1. stirring		a. a person who designs, makes, or sells hats
_____ 2. sloop		b. a rascal
_____ 3. aspiration		c. not having something needed, wanted, or expected
_____ 4. unaccountable		d. rousing; exciting
_____ 5. milliner		e. a sudden disclosure of something not previously realized
_____ 6. rapscallion		f. the act of continually treating in a cruel way
_____ 7. aristocrat		g. a type of sailboat
_____ 8. revelation		h. plots; secret schemes
_____ 9. agile		i. a member of the upper class
_____ 10. intrigues		j. a strong desire to achieve something
_____ 11. persecution		k. mentally quick; able to move quickly and easily
_____ 12. bereft		l. inexplicable; strange

Comprehension & Discussion Questions

1. Why did Amos particularly look forward to seeing General Washington?

_____

2. Why did General Washington send Benjamin Franklin to France?

_____

3. Was Ben's trip to France a success? Explain.

_____

4. Why were Amos's nerves on edge when at the home of Madame Helvetius?

_____

5. Who was Sophia? What did Amos promise to do for her?

_____

Follow-up Activities

1. In writing dialogue, it is a good idea to vary the verbs. Look through Chapter X. Find at least three verbs that are used in place of "said." Brainstorm and add many different words that could be used to replace the word "said."
2. In describing the French ladies' admiration for Benjamin Franklin, the author used the following simile: "They swarmed around him like flies around a honey-jar." Define the term simile. Create an original simile.

Chapters XII and XIII:
Plans and *The Battle of Versailles*

Vocabulary: Match the vocabulary word on the left with the definition on the right.

____ 1. reflection	a. men overly interested in their clothing and appearance
____ 2. gout	b. playful or funny actions
____ 3. infested	c. came together for a common purpose
____ 4. antics	d. an opinion formed after careful thought
____ 5. fops	e. short, curved swords
____ 6. prone	f. likely to act in a certain way
____ 7. cudgel	g. a disease marked by painful swelling of the joints
____ 8. motley	h. overrun in large numbers so as to be unpleasant or harmful
____ 9. rallied	i. composed of various, often unlike, parts
____ 10. fray	j. a heated dispute or contest
____ 11. cutlasses	k. a short, heavy club

Comprehension & Discussion Questions

1. What good news did Ben and Amos receive that was cause for celebration?

_____

2. Amos said the house was infested with hairdressers and shirtmakers. Why is the use of the word "infested" ironic?

_____

3. What caused the peasant rats to desert the battle?

_____

4. Who rescued Sophia's children from the Palace at Versailles?

_____

5. Why had Ben "lost a great deal of his popularity"?

_____

Follow-up Activities

1. Red said to Amos, "I had a winter at Valley Forge under Von Steuben...I know something of discipline." Explain who Baron Friedrich von Steuben was and describe his importance to the revolutionary cause.
2. When the sailor rats of John Paul Jones arrived, Amos thought, "Lafayette, we are here!" Explain who Lafayette was and describe his importance to the revolutionary cause.

Chapters XIV and XV:
Home and *Happy Birthday!*

Vocabulary: Match the vocabulary word on the left with the definition on the right.

____	1. gracious	a.	calm and serious in manner
____	2. downcast	b.	marked by kindness and courtesy
____	3. snubbed	c.	a slow, graceful dance
____	4. reception	d.	the point of highest dramatic interest
____	5. delegations	e.	being in a state of low confidence; dejected
____	6. threadbare	f.	made an attempt at; tried
____	7. meandered	g.	ignored; treated rudely
____	8. staid	h.	wandered
____	9. succumbed	i.	the act of welcoming
____	10. minuet	j.	yielded to force or pressure
____	11. essayed	k.	groups of persons chosen to represent others
____	12. climax	l.	shabby; extremely worn

Comprehension & Discussion Questions

1. How did Amos cheer Ben on their voyage home?

_____

2. Amos no longer wanted to accompany Ben to his dinners and committee meetings; however, he did not want to hurt his feelings. How did he solve his problem?

_____

3. What gifts did Amos's mother and father give to Ben?

_____

4. Ben had conflicting feelings about Amos's gift. Explain.

_____

5. How did Amos console Ben? What one bit of advice did he give him?

_____

Follow-up Activities

1. Did you enjoy this book? Write a letter to a friend explaining why you would or would not recommend it.
2. Read a traditional biography of Benjamin Franklin.

Thomas and Me

Pretend you are Thomas Edison's mouse (or other animal). Write a chapter for a book entitled *Thomas and Me.* In your chapter describe how you helped him invent something. Give your chapter a title.

Historical Fiction

In historical fiction true facts are mixed with fiction. Real names, dates, and settings help make the story seem more realistic. *Ben and Me,* by Robert Lawson, is an example of historical fiction.

Re-read the story. As you read, note which facts are historically true. List the historically true facts in the column on the left. List the fictional facts in the column on the right. Include at least ten facts in each column.

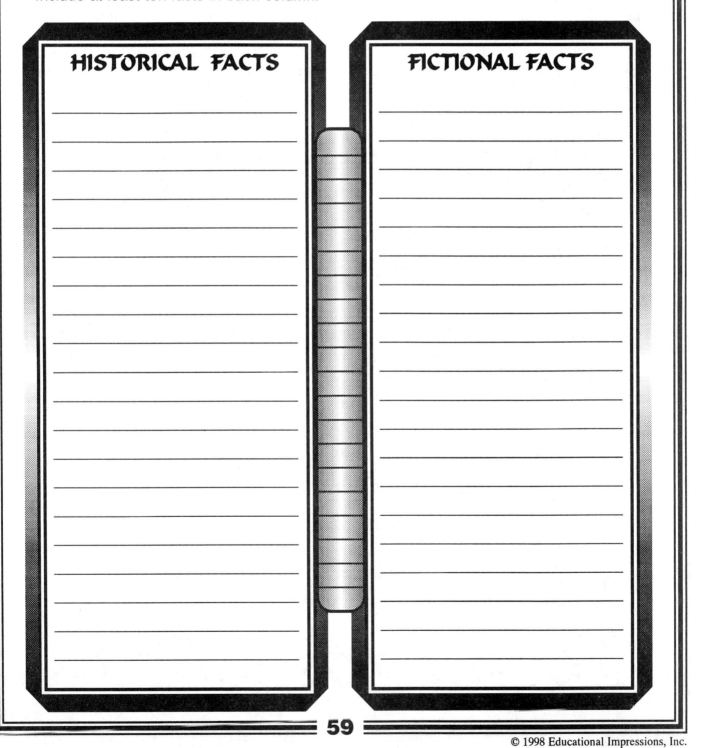

HISTORICAL FACTS

FICTIONAL FACTS

John Muir

Naturalist John Muir was born in Scotland on April 21, 1838. He and his family moved to the United States when John was eleven. They settled in Wisconsin and farmed the land, as they had done in their native country.

John Muir developed a strong love of nature. He spent a lot of time lobbying Congress. His goal was to convince Congress to designate the high country around Yosemite Valley, on the California-Nevada border, a national park. In 1890 his hard work paid off. Two years later he helped found the Sierra Club.

John Muir spent all of his adult life studying and writing about the wilderness. He loved the forests and mountains and all the plants and animals found there. He died on December 24, 1914.

A clerihew is a humorous biographical quatrain. The person is usually named in the first line. Create a clerihew about John Muir.

Choose a national park. Research it and create a travel brochure encouraging tourists to visit the park.

Create a National Park Scrambled-Word Game.

In 1908 President Theodore Roosevelt established Muir Woods Natural Monument in Muir's honor. Find out where Muir Woods is located.

The major attraction of the parks on the next page are their natural beauty and/or unique natural features. The National Park Service also includes military parks, battlefields, monuments, seashores, and other historical and recreational areas. Buck Island Reef Natural Monument is located in the U.S. Virgin Islands. Find out what is unique about this park area.

NOTE: You may use the list of national parks on the following page to help you with these activities.

National Parks

The following is a partial listing of United States National Parks. The major attraction of these parks are their natural beauty and/or unique natural features. The National Park Service also includes park areas that are primarily historical or recreational.

NATIONAL PARK	STATE
North Cascades National Park	Washington
Olympic National Park	Washington
Mount Rainier National Park	Washington
Crater Lake National Park	Oregon
Lassen Volcanic National Park	California
Yosemite National Park	California
Kings Canyon National Park	California
Redwoods National Park	California
Sequoia National Park	California
Glacier National Park	Montana
Yellowstone National Park	Wyoming
Grand Teton National Park	Wyoming
Arches National Park	Utah
Canyonlands National Park	Utah
Capital Reef National Park	Utah
Bryce Canyon National Park	Utah
Zion National Park	Utah
Rocky Canyon National Park	Colorado
Mesa Verde National Park	Colorado
Grand Canyon National Park	Arizona
Petrified Forest National Park	Arizona
Carlsbad Caverns National Park	New Mexico
Theodore Roosevelt National Park	North Dakota
Voyageurs National Park	Minnesota
Wind Cave National Park	South Dakota
Badlands National Park	South Dakota
Hot Springs National Park	Arkansas
Guadeloupe Mountains National Park	Texas
Big Bend National Park	Texas
Isle Royal National Park	Michigan
Mammoth Cave National Park	Kentucky
Shenandoah National Park	Virginia
Great Smoky Mountains National Park	Tennessee
Everglades National Park	Florida
Acadia National Park	Maine
Denali National Park	Alaska
Mount McKinley National Park	Alaska
Haleakala National Park	Hawaii
Hawaii Volcanoes National Park	Hawaii
Virgin Islands National Park	St. John, VI

OUR ENVIRONMENT

The first Earth Day was observed on April 22, 1970. In honor of Earth Day, think about all we can do to help preserve Earth and its environment— its atmosphere, mountains, lakes, oceans, forests, and wildlife!

Waste Not, Want Not

Waste disposal is a very big problem. Years ago, much of the solid waste we disposed of was placed in open dumps. These dumps were a source of air and water pollution. Luckily, they have been replaced by sanitary landfills. In these landfills, waste is compressed, and each layer is covered with clay or another substance that doesn't allow fluid to pass through. Although far from perfect, the landfills are a great improvement over the open dumps.

Many towns and cities have recycling programs. Residents are asked to separate their garbage by material. For example, the town might ask that residents separate newspapers, glass, plastic, and tin.

In addition to participating in the local recycling program, individuals can help by reducing the amount of garbage they generate: by reusing whatever they can, by limiting disposable items, and by buying recyclable products and products with the least amount of waste.

Brainstorm and think of all the things you, your family, your classmates, and your teacher could do to lesson the amount of garbage you generate.

At Home	At School

Fossil Fuels

Electric power, probably more than anything else, has been responsible for the high standard of living enjoyed by the industrialized nations of the world. Electricity is produced by changing some other form of energy. The mechanical energy of falling water can be converted into electrical energy. The heat energy of fossil fuels, such as coal, petroleum (oil), and natural gas can also be converted into electrical energy. Demand for electricity has increased steadily during the twentieth century. It promises to keep on increasing because of our continued desire to raise our standard of living and also because of our ever-growing population!

Most of the energy consumed in the United States comes from fossil fuels. Fossil fuels are formed from the remains of plant and animal life of a previous geological time. We use these fossil fuels in many ways. Coal, oil, and natural gas are all burned directly in homes and other buildings to heat them. Coal and oil are burned in power plants to produce electricity. As gasoline, petroleum moves our cars, buses, trucks, and other vehicles. Petroleum is used to manufacture many products, such as plastic items, crayons, and polyester clothing. Natural gas is used for cooking. There are environmental problems associated with the burning of all of these resources. Also, oil, upon which we are most dependent, is relatively scarce and exhaustible.

It is in our best interests to conserve energy in every way possible. The problems associated with fossil fuels also emphasize the need to develop and use renewable energy sources. These sources are all derived either directly or indirectly from solar energy. Renewable energy sources include direct solar energy, hydropower, geothermal energy, and wind energy. They are practically inexhaustible and they do not affect the environment like the burning of fossil fuels does.

NOTE: This page was taken from *Our Environment,* written by Rebecca Stark and published by Educational Impressions, Inc.

Conserving Energy

Think of many different ways to conserve energy.

What can you and your family members do at home to conserve energy?

_____

_____

_____

_____

_____

_____

What can you, your classmates, your teachers, and your principal do at school to conserve energy?

_____

_____

_____

_____

_____

_____

_____

_____

What can your mother and/or father do at work to conserve energy?

_____

_____

_____

_____

_____

_____

_____

_____

Put a check next to those things you, your friends, or your family members are already doing in an attempt to conserve energy.

Tropical Rain Forests

Earth's tropical rain forests are disappearing at an alarming rate. The main cause is slash-and-burn farming. Ecologists worry about the loss of our rain forests for several reasons.

One reason for concern is that the loss of the trees throws off the balance of carbon dioxide and oxygen in the atmosphere. Because trees take in carbon dioxide and give off oxygen, the loss of the trees puts more carbon dioxide into the atmosphere. Many scientists believe this will cause global warming.

Another reason ecologists worry about the destruction of rain forests is that these rain forests are teeming with life. Many plants and animals found nowhere else are being destroyed! Ecologists don't like to see any plant or animal species become extinct; however, their concern for the loss of these tropical plants is even greater. Several drugs have been derived from plants found only in the rain forests. Among them are drugs used to treat malaria, Hodgkin's disease, glaucoma, hypertension, and rheumatoid arthritis.

Rain forests are a very important part of Earth's environment. It will take worldwide cooperation to save them!

The Greenhouse Effect

Many scientists believe that too much carbon dioxide will lead to global warming. They say that the burning of fossil fuels and the destruction of forests are two main reasons for the increase. "Greenhouse effect" is the term used to describe the way in which carbon dioxide and some other gases heat the atmosphere.

Explain what is meant by the greenhouse effect.

_____

_____

_____

_____

_____

_____

Draw a chart that clarifies your explanation.

The National Cancer Institute has identified about 3,000 plants as having anti-cancer properties. About 70% of those plants are native to the rain forest. With this in mind, write a letter to a farmer who is engaging in slash-and-burn farming of the rain forest.

Biologist Rachel Carson was best known for her book *Silent Spring*. Find out what the book was about. Write a two- or three-sentence summary of the book.

Design a poster to encourage people to help Save Our Rain Forests.

The main areas of equatorial rain forest are the Amazon lowlands, the Congo lowlands (with a coastal zone extending from Nigeria to Guinea), Sumatra and other parts of Indonesia, and several Pacific Islands. Locate these places on a map. HINT: Think about the meaning of "equatorial."

Scrambled Animals of the Amazon

About one-third of all the species of plants and animals found on earth are thought to inhabit the complex ecosystem of the Amazon rain forest. Many haven't even been named. Unscramble these words to find out the names of a few animals found there.

1. AMAZNO APRRTO _____
2. CSALRTE AMCWA _____
3. LWO-AFCDE OMNEKY _____
4. OBA COSNTRCITRO _____
5. MUPA _____
6. UGINAA _____
7. GAJAUR _____
8. ERTE RFOG _____
9. ATPRI _____
10. MUHMINGRBID _____
11. WTO-OTED LSOHT _____
12. ANSLI _____

Life in the African Rain Forest

There are four layers in the African Rain Forest. From top to bottom they are the emergent layer, the canopy, the understory, and the floor. Each layer is home to a different set of creatures.

The following animals can be found in the African Rain Forest. Put them into groups. Try to think of many unusual groups as well as more common ones. There must be at least two items to a group, and an animal may be included in more than one group. Two groups have been started for you. Have fun!

woodpecker	striped squirrel	Diana monkey
eagle	viper	skipper butterfly
mandrill	python	African gray parrot
chimpanzee	rhinoceros beetle	Congo peafowl
owl	gorilla	forest hog
tree frog	crocodile	civet
leopard	snail	bongo
red Colobus monkey	elephant	checkered elephant shrew

BIRDS
woodpecker

HAVE PROPER NOUN AS PART OF NAME
Diana monkey

© 1998 Educational Impressions, Inc.

The Lorax

by Dr. Seuss

A good book to read in honor of Earth Day is *The Lorax,* by Dr. Seuss.

Questions and Activities Based on Bloom's Taxonomy

These questions and activities should be completed after reading the book.

KNOWLEDGE

1. In what form is this book written?
2. Who narrates most of the book?
3. What did the Once-ler sell?

COMPREHENSION

4. Why did the Once-ler cut down the first Truffula tree?
5. Who popped out of the stump of the cut-down Truffula tree?
6. Why did the Lorax have to speak for the trees?

APPLICATION

7. Make a chart that shows why each creature had to leave the land.
8. Create a chart to encourage people to conserve our forests.
9. Create a chart showing the parts of a tree.

ANALYSIS

10. Compare and contrast the land before and after the Once-ler arrived.
11. Why was the Once-ler out of business? What might he have done differently to stay in business?
12. Analyze the importance of trees to our environment.

SYNTHESIS

13. Create an environmental ABC's in which you describe ways to improve our environment.
14. Think of another name for a Thnead.
15. Write a sequel to the story. What does the boy do with the Truffula seeds? What are the results?

EVALUATION

16. Describe the mood at the beginning of the book.
17. Describe the mood at the end of the book.
18. Evaluate the one-word message left by the Lorax.

Math Fun

April is Mathematics Education Month. Here are some fun things to do using your mathematics skills.

SITUATION NO. 1: At the Circus

You are a ten-year-old boy.

You, your mother, your father, your 13-year-old sister, your eight-year-old brother, and your grandmother want to go to the circus.

Ticket prices are as follows:

	ADULTS (12 & over)	CHILD
SPECIAL UP-FRONT SECTION	$25.00	$20.00
MAIN SECTION	$18.00	$15.00
BALCONY	$13.00	$11.00

How much will the tickets cost if you all sit in the special up-front section?

How much will the tickets cost if everyone sits up front except your father and mother, who sit in the main section?

How much will your family save if you all sit in the balcony instead of in the special up-front section?

SITUATION NO. 2: At the Ball Game

You are at a baseball game with your two friends, Amy and Scott.

You, Amy, and Scott each have a different amount of money to spend on souvenirs and refreshments.

    You have $5.40.
    Amy has $9.00.
    Scott has $12.65.

The hawkers (people who try to peddle things by calling out) are selling the following goods at these prices:

Soda:	$1.50
Hot dogs:	$3.00
Cotton candy:	$ .75
Peanuts:	$1.75
Popcorn:	$1.00
Souvenir books:	$2.50
Baseballs:	$2.00

If you buy a soda and a hot dog, what else can you buy? How much money will you have left if you buy it?

How much money would someone need to buy one of each item? Does anyone in your group have enough money to buy one of each? Would he or she have any money left? If so, how much?

Suppose you wanted to buy peanuts, a soda, a souvenir book, and a baseball. How much money would you have to borrow from your friends?

SITUATION NO. 3: At the Pizza Parlor

Six friends go to the pizza parlor and order three pies.

Each pie has eight pieces.

How many pieces are there in all?

If each friend has an equal number of pieces, how many will each have?

Suppose one friend is not very hungry. She wants only one piece. Another friend wants three pieces. How many can each of the other four friends have if they all have an equal amount?

It is time to pay for the pizzas. The friends decide each will pay according to the number of pieces he or she ate. Each pie costs $10.00. How much will each friend pay?

	No. of Pieces Eaten	AMOUNT
Friend No. 1	2 pieces	_____
Friend No. 2	3 pieces	_____
Friend No. 3	5 pieces	_____
Friend No. 4	6 pieces	_____
Friend No. 5	4 pieces	_____
Friend No. 6	4 pieces	_____

What is the total bill? _____

EXTRA: Suppose each leaves a 15% tip. How much will each leave? (Round off to the nearest penny.)

		TIP
Friend No. 1	2 pieces	_____
Friend No. 2	3 pieces	_____
Friend No. 3	5 pieces	_____
Friend No. 4	6 pieces	_____
Friend No. 5	4 pieces	_____
Friend No. 6	4 pieces	_____

Spring Garden

In many places spring is a good time to plant a garden. The following are some things that may be found in a vegetable garden. Put them into groups. Try to think of many unusual groups as well as more common ones. There must be at least two items to a group, and an item may be included in more than one group. Two groups have been started for you. Have fun!

basket
birds
cabbage
carrots
corn
cucumber
fence
gardener
hoe

lettuce
lima beans
peas
peppers
pumpkins
rabbit
radishes
scallions
scarecrow

seeds
shovel
soil
squash
string beans
tomatoes
turnips
watering can
weeds

TWO-SYLLABLE WORDS
Basket

TOOLS
Hoe

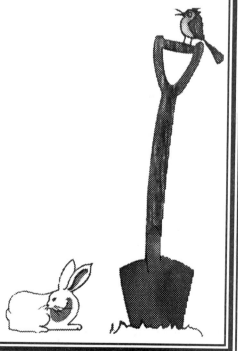

Plants

Plants are living things.

Without plants, people and animals would have no food to eat. It's true that many people and animals eat other animals; however, those other animals rely on plants for their diet.

Plants help us in many ways. List all the things you can think of that plants give us besides food. Try to think of both usual and unusual answers.

Now draw a picture of one of the things you listed.

Parts of a Flowering Plant

A plant has four main parts. Each part has a different function, or job.
The main parts of a plant are the roots, the stem, the leaves, and the flowers.

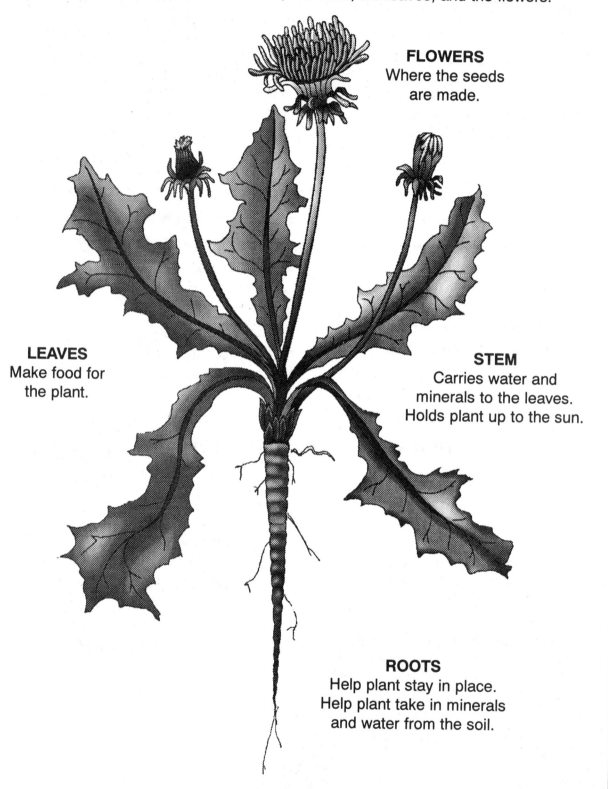

FLOWERS
Where the seeds
are made.

LEAVES
Make food for
the plant.

STEM
Carries water and
minerals to the leaves.
Holds plant up to the sun.

ROOTS
Help plant stay in place.
Help plant take in minerals
and water from the soil.

Most flowers make seeds. To do this they need a special dusty substance called pollen. Draw a chart that shows some ways pollen is spread.

Create a maze for a younger child in which a bee must find its way to the pollen.

Sometimes the area surrounding the seeds is quite large. Large seed containers are called fruit. Brainstorm and list many different kinds of fruit.

Use the list you created in the brainstorming activity to create a scrambled-word game.

Use the list you created in the brainstorming activity to create a word-search puzzle.

79

Wanderers of the Sky: Birds

Every year many birds fly south for the winter. In the spring, they fly back to their northern homes; there they build their nests and raise their young.

Time to Rise

A birdie with a yellow bill
Hopped upon my windowsill,
Cocked his shining eye and said:
"Ain't you 'shamed, you sleepy head!"

—Robert Louis Stevenson

The above quatrain by Robert Louis Stevenson has an *aabb* rhyme scheme. Write an original quatrain (4-lined poem) about birds in general or about a particular kind of bird. Your quatrain may have an *aabb*, *abab*, *abcb*, or *abba* rhyme scheme. Give your poem a title.

Illustrate your poem.

Syllogisms

A **syllogism** is a form of deductive reasoning. It consists of a major premise, a minor premise, and a conclusion. To be valid, the conclusion must be in **agreement with** and **based upon** the previous statements.

The following is an example of a valid syllogism:
  (A) All birds have feathers. **(Major Premise)**
  (B) The robin is a bird. **(Minor Premise)**
  (C) Therefore, the robin has feathers. **(Conclusion)**

Complete each of the following syllogisms with a valid conclusion:

1. (A) Only birds have feathers.
    (B) The robin has feathers.
    (C) Therefore, _____.

2. (A) All birds are warm-blooded; their temperature stays about the same.
    (B) The parrot is a bird.
    (C) Therefore, _____.

3. (A) All birds belong to the class *Aves*.
    (B) The mockingbird is a bird.
    (C) Therefore, _____.

Decide whether the following syllogisms are valid or invalid. If invalid, explain why.

4. (A) All birds have a backbone.
    (B) The camel has a backbone.
    (C) Therefore, the camel is a bird. _____

    _____

5. (A) Most birds are unable to care for themselves shortly after hatching.
    (B) Ducklings are able to care for themselves shortly after hatching.
    (C) Therefore, ducks are not birds. _____

    _____

6. (A) Birds give birth to their young by laying eggs.
    (B) Snakes lay eggs.
    (C) Therefore, snakes are birds. _____

    _____

Bird Crossword

ACROSS

2. Thrush and other ___birds have four long toes with long nails to grasp the branches.
4. Ducks and other birds that can care for themselves shortly after hatching are covered with this.
6. Chickens and turkeys belong to this group.
8. Birds of prey have sharp claws called ___.
10. Most birds use these to fly.
11. The dodo is ___; it no longer exists.
15. To move seasonally from one location to another.
17. This red-breasted bird is a sign of spring in many places.
18. Water birds like ducks and swans have ___ feet.
19. This flightless marine bird lives in the cool regions of the Southern Hemisphere.
20. Like mammals, birds are ___-___.
22. A bird has a ___ that extends beyond the main part of its body.
23. Eagles, hawks, and falcons are birds of ___.
24. Birds and other vertebrates have one.
25. Most birds can do this.
26. This very large flightless bird is found in Africa.

DOWN

1. An example of a wading bird.
3. A place where a bird incubates eggs.
5. Scientist who studies birds.
7. This bird imitates the songs of other birds.
9. Baby birds hatch from these.
12. Birds have ___ eyes and ears.
13. The male of this species is bright red.
14. Only birds have these.
16. Another word for a bird's bill.
18. It has a chisel-like beak to drill tree barks.
20. "The early bird catches the ___."
21. The routes taken by migrating birds are called ___.

82

A War on Polio

Virologist Dr. Jonas Salk was the first to develop a vaccine for the prevention of paralytic poliomyelitis. He was the director of the University of Pittsburgh's Virus Research Laboratory. He and his associates had been working on polio research for about five years when he finally announced that his vaccine was ready for mass testing.

Never before had such a project been undertaken. The mass vaccinations began on April 26, 1954. Almost two million children between the ages of six and nine were inoculated! The testing required the work of over 100,000 doctors, nurses, and teachers and about 200,000 non-professional volunteers.

In 1955 virologist Dr. Albert Sabin developed another form of the vaccine. How did his vaccine differ from that of Dr. Salk?

Research the effects of paralytic poliomyletis. Create a poem about Dr. Salk.

"Poliomyletis" is a big word. How many little words (3 or more letters) can you form using its letters? Do not use the "s" to form plurals.

Research and report on another scientist. Write a paragraph describing his or her greatest achievement.

Easter

Easter is always celebrated on a Sunday. For Western Christians the date falls between March 22 and April 25. For members of the Eastern Orthodox Church the date can be the same as for the Western Church, or it can fall one, four, or five weeks later.

Draw or paint a picture of an Easter Egg.

Plan an Easter Basket for a kindergarten girl or boy. What will you include?

Create a bunny mask using construction paper, glue, pipe cleaners, and other materials.

Plan an Easter-Egg Hunt.

Whom will you invite?

Where will you hide the eggs?

Will there be prizes? If so, what will you give away?

Will you serve refreshments? If so, what will you serve?

84

Passover

Passover is an 8-day Jewish holiday that is observed during the Hebrew month of Nisan (15 to 22). Sometimes this falls in March and sometimes it falls in April. The holiday celebrates the time, thousands of years ago, when the Jewish slaves were freed from the harsh rule of the cruel pharaoh of Egypt.

See if you can match the items on the left with their definitions on the right.

1. Haggadah
2. Pharaoh
3. Moses
4. Matzo
5. Seder
6. Exodus

A. Unleavened bread
P. The book used to tell the story of Passover.
C. The Passover meal and service
H. The departure of the Israelites (Jews) from Egypt
E. Ruler of ancient Egypt
S. Led the Jews out of Egypt

If you write the letters in order of your answers, you will learn another name for Passover.

___ ___ ___ ___ ___ ___

Symbols of Passover

On every seder table there are a plate of matzos and a seder plate with the symbols of Passover placed on it. (*Seder* really means "order of the service.")

The **matzo** is a reminder that when the Jews left Egypt, they had no time to bake bread. The sun baked the raw dough into hard crackers.

Parsley or another green is dipped into salt water as a reminder of spring and life. This is to show gratitude for the products of the earth.

The **bitter herbs, or maror,** are a reminder of the bitterness of slavery.

Charoset, a mixture of chopped apples and walnuts, looks a little like clay. It is a reminder of the clay used by the Jews to make the bricks for the Pharaoh's cities and buildings. The bitter herbs are dipped into this sweet mixture as a sign of hope.

The **roasted egg** is a reminder of spring.

The **roasted bone** is also a symbol of spring. It is a reminder of the lamb which was sacrificed on the eve of the Exodus from Egypt and later eaten with the matzo.

On Passover it is customary to recline at the service. Do you know or can you guess why?

_____

_____

_____

Arbor Day

Arbor Day, an annual tree-planting day, was first observed on April 10, 1872, in Nebraska. Its original goal was to beautify public grounds. The governor of the state, Julius Sterling Morgan, suggested the holiday and its name. In 1885 Arbor Day became a legal holiday in Nebraska. The date of its observance was set at April 22, Morgan's birthday.

Over the years, both the scope of the observance and its objective grew. The observance of Arbor Day spread throughout the United States. Today we stress the importance of forestry and reforesting wastelands as well as beautification. Most states observe the holiday on the last Friday in April.

TREES

Trees are the largest plants on Earth. Many are also the oldest. They can live for hundreds of years. Some species even live for thousands of years!

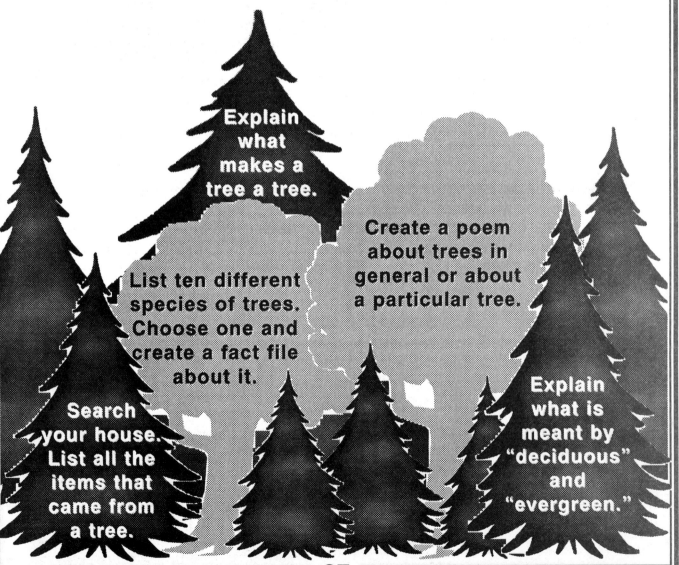

Explain what makes a tree a tree.

Create a poem about trees in general or about a particular tree.

List ten different species of trees. Choose one and create a fact file about it.

Search your house. List all the items that came from a tree.

Explain what is meant by "deciduous" and "evergreen."

The Giving Tree
by Shel Silverstein

In honor of Arbor Day, read *The Giving Tree,* written and illustrated by Shel Silverstein.

Questions and Activities Based on Bloom's Taxonomy
These questions and activities should be completed after reading the book.

KNOWLEDGE
1. What kind of tree was it?
2. What did the young boy do with the leaves?
3. How did the young boy use the branches?

COMPREHENSION
4. How did the tree solve the older boy's money problem?
5. How did the tree help the boy get a house when he was a young man?
6. How did the tree help the boy fulfill his dream of sailing away as an older man?

APPLICATION
7. Suggest other ways the boy might have obtained money to buy things and to have fun.
8. Draw a picture of an activity that makes you happy.
9. Draw a diagram of a tree. Label its parts.

ANALYSIS
10. Create a chart that shows how the relationship between the boy and the tree changed over the years.
11. In your opinion, who got the most out of this relationship? Explain.
12. Look up the terms "symbiotic" and "parasitic." Tell which best describes their relationship and explain why.

SYNTHESIS
13. Think of something the boy might have done for the tree.
14. Create a conversation between the boy (at any age) and the tree in which the boy asks for something else.
15. As the tree, write an entry for your diary the day after the boy cut down your trunk.

EVALUATION
16. As the old man, write a thank-you note to the tree expressing your appreciation for all it has done for you throughout your life.
17. Do you think the boy should have accepted the tree's offer to have its trunk cut down?
18. Judge the appropriateness of the title of the book. Create a new title.

National Wildlife Week

The last week in April is National Wildlife Week. This is a good time to think about animals that are extinct—those that no longer exist. Some examples of extinct animals are the mammoth, the saber-toothed tiger, the dinosaurs, the dodo, and the passenger pigeon. In the 1800s between five and nine **billion** passenger pigeons inhabited the eastern parts of North America! The western settlers slaughtered them by the millions. Now there are none!

It is also time to think about endangered species, animals in danger of becoming extinct. See if you can find the names of these endangered animals in the word-search puzzle. Remember to look up, down, forwards, backwards, and diagonally!

- elephant
- pigmy hippopotamus
- gila monster
- Asiatic lion
- giant anteater
- mountain gorilla
- Siberian tiger
- California condor

- drill
- proboscis monkey
- snow leopard
- humpback whale
- Bornean orangutan
- red-tailed parrot
- bighorn sheep
- Komodo dragon

P	S	B	O	R	N	E	A	N	O	R	A	N	G	U	T	A	N	R	N	G
R	I	T	N	A	H	P	E	L	E	A	S	T	K	I	O	N	A	E	L	I
O	B	G	W	L	W	E	B	S	S	I	I	T	O	E	F	W	A	T	T	A
B	E	I	M	I	O	N	A	N	D	I	A	G	M	E	R	S	N	S	O	N
O	R	A	R	Y	L	I	D	C	E	M	T	H	O	A	E	G	H	N	R	T
S	I	E	L	W	H	I	R	Q	H	O	I	W	D	R	L	T	D	O	R	A
C	A	U	O	D	N	I	R	E	N	K	C	O	O	S	A	D	B	M	A	N
I	N	H	L	Y	L	E	P	D	D	X	L	A	D	R	H	R	E	A	P	T
S	T	V	I	H	I	G	Y	P	E	S	I	R	R	A	W	A	Z	L	D	E
M	I	T	T	I	T	K	A	U	O	Q	O	F	A	S	K	P	L	I	E	A
O	G	D	J	Y	T	F	M	Y	S	P	N	F	G	A	C	O	A	G	L	T
N	E	E	L	D	L	I	S	E	T	R	O	R	O	M	A	E	W	P	I	E
K	R	L	N	D	R	I	L	L	I	E	L	T	N	I	B	L	E	R	A	R
E	M	I	R	T	M	E	A	S	T	H	S	O	A	N	P	W	A	E	T	K
Y	L	A	X	H	A	P	V	W	Y	O	S	U	L	M	M	O	O	I	D	N
M	O	U	N	T	A	I	N	G	O	R	I	L	L	A	U	N	T	L	E	I
N	O	P	E	E	H	S	N	R	O	H	G	I	B	U	H	S	D	N	R	E
C	A	L	I	F	O	R	N	I	A	C	O	N	D	O	R	S	T	I	K	B

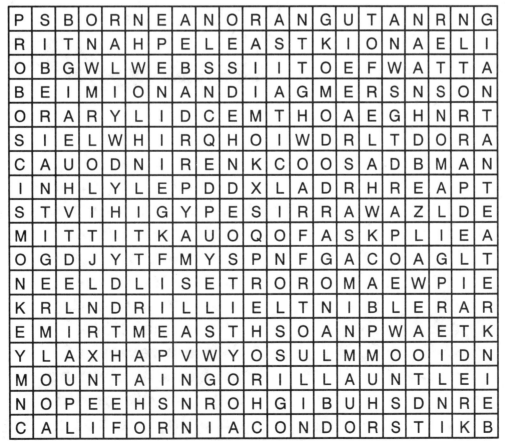

Reading Is Fun

The last week in April is Reading Is Fun Week!

Design a book jacket for your favorite book.

What is your favorite book? Who wrote it? If it has pictures, who illustrated it?

Read another book by the author of your favorite book. You may need to ask your teacher or your librarian for help.

Draw a picture of a favorite scene in your book. Write a paragraph explaining what is happening.

Take a poll of "favorite" books in your class. Choose one of the books chosen by your classmates that you have never read. Read that book. Write a review of that book explaining why you did or did not enjoy the book.

Maryland

One of the thirteen original colonies, Maryland became a state when it ratified the Constitution on April 28, 1788.

Match the names on the left with the descriptions on the right. Write the letter that comes before the description. The letters will spell the name of an important city.

___ 1. Old Line State & Free State   (I) Professional baseball team

___ 2. Annapolis   (B) State's nicknames

___ 3. White oak   (M) State flower

___ 4. The Mason and Dixon Line   (T) Border between Maryland and Pennsylvania

___ 5. The Baltimore Orioles   (A) Capital of Maryland

___ 6. Black-eyed Susan   (R) Known for its oysters

___ 7. Ocean City   (O) Popular beach resort

___ 8. Chesapeake Bay   (L) State tree

___ 9. Fort McHenry   (E) Its bombing inspired the writing of the "Star-Spangled Banner"

Louisiana

Louisiana became the eighteenth state on April 30, 1812.

Use the clues about Louisiana on the left to complete the names and terms on the right. Then write the letters you have filled in, keeping them in the same order. The letters will spell the name of one of Louisiana's state songs.

1. State insect   H O N E __ B E E

2. State Capital   B A T __ N R O __ G E

3. City in SW Louisiana   L __ K E C H A __ L __ S

4. State flower   __ A G N O L I A

5. State tree   B A L D C __ P R E S __

6. State motto   __ __ I O N, J U __ T I C E, AND C O N F I D E N C E

7. City in NW Louisiana   S __ R E V E P O R T

8. State nickname   P E L __ C A __ S T A T E

9. City in SE Louisiana   N __ W O R L E A N S

The name of the state song is

_____

NOTE: The other state song is "Give Me Louisiana."

Categories

Fill in each category: food, animals, cities (include state or foreign country), and countries. Be sure to start with the proper letter: S,P,R,I,N, or G. Score one point for each correct answer that another person also has. Score two points for an answer no one else has. You may put more than one answer in each square.

	FOOD	ANIMALS	CITIES	COUNTRIES
S				
P				
R				
I				
N				
G				

Springtime Senses

Think about each of our five senses: sight, smell, hearing, touch, and taste. Brainstorm and list as many things as you can for each category.

SIGHTS OF SPRING

_____
_____
_____
_____
_____
_____
_____

SOUNDS OF SPRING

_____
_____
_____
_____
_____
_____
_____

TASTES OF SPRING

_____
_____
_____
_____
_____
_____
_____

SMELLS OF SPRING

_____
_____
_____
_____
_____
_____
_____

TOUCH SENSATIONS OF SPRING

_____   _____
_____   _____
_____   _____

94

An Acrostic

In an acrostic poem the first letter of each line spells out the name of a person, place, thing, or idea. Use the lists you created about springtime senses to help you write an acrostic about spring. Then illustrate your poem.

SPRINGTIME

S _____

P _____

R _____

I _____

N _____

G _____

T _____

I _____

M _____

E _____

95

A Haiku

Haiku is a Japanese form of poetry with three lines. The lines do not have to rhyme, but they do have to follow a set pattern.

This is the pattern:

    line 1 = 5 syllables

    line 2 = 7 syllables

    line 3 = 5 syllables

Here is an example of a haiku about summer:

Summer

Children home from school,

Playing, singing in the sun.

Having so much fun.

Create a haiku about spring.	Create a haiku about April.
Spring	*April*
_____	_____
_____	_____
_____	_____
_____	_____

=== 96 ===

© 1998 Educational Impressions, Inc.

Spring Sports Logic

Part I: Analogies

Complete these analogies about spring sports. The relationship of the third term to the fourth term should be the same as the relationship of the first term to the second term.

1. club : golf :: _____ : tennis

2. baseball : diamond :: _____ : court

3. hit : softball :: kick : _____

4. big : soccer ball :: little : _____

5. individual : golf:: _____ : baseball

Part II: Which One Does Not Belong

Think about all four terms in each set. Decide which of the four does not belong and circle it. Explain why you chose that term.

6. hole-in-one   tee   iron   racket

_____

7. love   net   putt   serve

_____

8. goalie   forward   birdie   foul

_____

9. bat   glove   helmet   offside

_____

10. tobogganing   soccer   softball   golf

_____

A Different Kind of Puzzle

Use the clues to help you decipher these "word" puzzles.

EXAMPLE: If you had a lot of free time, you might want to take one.

TRIPTRIPTRIPTRIPTRIP

TRIPTRIPTHE WORLDTRIPTRIP

TRIPTRIPTRIPTRIPTRIP

ANSWER: Trip Around the World

---

1. Spring fever leads to this.

LOFALLINGVE

Answer: _____

---

2. This might describe someone with spring fever.

LOVE

Answer: _____

---

3. What someone might be doing during a spring shower.

THESINGINGRAIN

Answer: _____

---

4. You might see one in a spring garden.

BLROSEOOM

Answer: _____

---

5. You probably won't need any in the spring.

WEAR

LONG

Answer: _____

---

6. A home-run hitter might do this.

RUNRUNRUNRUN
RUNTHE BASESRUN
RUNRUNRUNRUN

Answer: _____

---

7. Every golfer wants one.

ONHOLEE

Answer: _____

---

8. A passenger fell off the cruise ship and someone shouted this.

MAN
BOARD

Answer: _____

Now create two original "word" puzzles. Exchange with classmates to solve.

Design a Flag

Decorative flags have become very popular in many locales. Design a flag with an April or a spring theme. You may use other paper and change the shape if you wish.

April Crossword

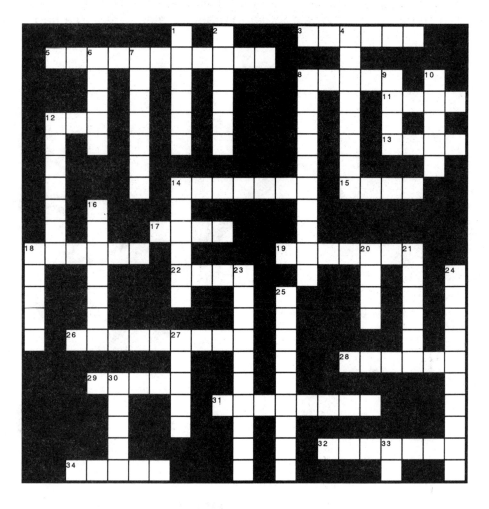

ACROSS

3. First name of 28 Across.
5. English dramatist and poet born in 1564.
8. Birds use these to fly.
11. *Ben and Me* is told from his point of view.
12. Acronym for World Health Organization.
13. 31 Across used one in his experiments with lightning.
14. His paintings were published in *The Birds of America*.
15. First name of 12 Down.
17. Plant part that carries water and minerals to the leaves.
18. What people play on April Fools' Day.
19. First name and middle initial of 8 Down.
22. Naturalist who convinced Congress to designate Yosemite a national park.
26. Third President of the United States.
28. Author of *Ben and Me*.
29. Unleavened bread eaten on Passover.
31. He wrote *Poor Richard's Almanac*.
32. A gorilla or a chimp.
34. He spoke for the trees in a book by Dr. Seuss.

DOWN

1. Season in April in the Northern Hemisphere.
2. First name of first African-American baseball player to play in major leagues.
4. First name of 31 Across
6. He broke Babe Ruth's home-run record.
7. A species that no longer exists is this.
8. He founded the Tuskegee Institute.
9. First to develop a vaccine to prevent polio.
10. He assassinated President Lincoln.
12. Known for *An American Dictionary of the English Language*.
14. Season in April in the Southern Hemisphere.
16. To extract useful materials and use again.
18. A haiku has ___ lines.
20. You might color or decorate some on Easter.
21. First name of 26 Across.
23. A tropical woodland with much rainfall and very tall trees.
25. Franklin wanted to prove it was electricity.
27. They help plants take minerals from the soil.
30. ___ Day is a tree-planting holiday.
33. Annapolis is its capital (postal abbreviation).

100

April Clip Art

April

SUNDAY	MONDAY	TUESDAY	WEDNESDAY	THURSDAY	FRIDAY	SATURDAY

Baby Animals

Many farm animals have babies in the spring. Enlarge or reduce these forms and use them to decorate worksheets, bulletin boards, awards, and so on. You might want to have the children copy original poems or stories onto the forms for an attractive display of their work.

Bibliography

Clark, Margaret Goff. *John Muir, Friend of Nature.* New York: Thomas Y. Crowell, 1973.

Faber, Harold and Doris Faber. *American Heroes of the 20th Century.* New York: Random House, 1967.

Frisky, Margaret. *Space Shuttles.* Chicago: Children's Press, 1982.

Graves, Charles P. *John Muir.* New York: Thomas Y. Crowell Company, 1973.

Jaffe, Charlotte and Barbara Doherty. *Shiloh L-I-T Guide.* Hawthorne, New Jersey: Educational Impressions, 1993.

Kane, Joseph Nathan. *Famous First Facts, Fourth Edition.* New York: The H. Wilson Company, 1981.

McKissack, Patricia and Fred McKissack. *The Story of Booker T. Washington.* Chicago: Children's Press, 1991.

Naylor, Phyllis Reynolds. *Shiloh.* New York: Dell Publishing, 1991.

Pallas, Stella. *A Thinking Cat's Guide to Birds.* Hawthorne, New Jersey: Educational Impressions, Inc., 1991.

Patterson, Dr. Francine. *Koko's Kitten.* New York: Scholastic, Inc., 1985.

___.*Koko's Kitten.* New York: Scholastic, Inc., 1987.

Patterson, Lillie G. *Booker T. Washington.* Champaign, Illinois: Garrard Publishing Company, 1962.

Seuss, Dr. *The Lorax.* New York: Random House, 1971.

Silverstein, Shel. *The Giving Tree.* New York: Harper Collins Publishers, 1964.

Stark, Rebecca. *Birds.* Hawthorne, New Jersey: Educational Impressions, Inc., 1990.

___. *Psychology.* Hawthorne, New Jersey: Educational Impressions, Inc., 1986.

Thomas Jefferson and His World. Editors of American Heritage. New York: Harper and Row, 1960.

Wade, Linda. *James Monroe.* Hawthorne, New Jersey: January Productions, Inc., 1993.

___. *Thomas Jefferson.* Hawthorne, New Jersey: January Productions, Inc., 1993.

VIDEO
Discovering Maps and Globes. Hawthorne, New Jersey: January Productions, Inc., 1990.

Answers and Background Information

Background information and answers are given as appropriate. Many activities call for original, creative answers. Answers are not given for those.

(Not Just) Openers: (pages 7-14)

Apr. 4: Dorothea Dix crusaded to improve conditions in prisons. She was especially concerned about the mentally ill, who were chained to chairs and integrated with vicious criminals. Because of her efforts, reforms were made both in the United States and abroad. Laws were passed that required the mentally ill to be placed in hospitals, not prisons.

Apr. 5: The Joint Chiefs of Staff is the most important military advisory group of the United States. It is composed of the chiefs of the Army, Navy, and Air Force and sometimes the commandant of the Marines.

Apr. 6: Four Eskimos and one African-American, Matthew Henson, accompanied Peary on his expedition. Some accounts say that Henson, Peary's assistant, actually reached the pole 45 minutes before Peary.

Apr. 7: WHO is an acronym that stands for World Health Organization. It is part of the United Nations. Its three general purposes are to provide research services and to disseminate the information; to help control epidemic and endemic disease through vaccination programs, instruction regarding antibiotics and insecticides, assistance in setting up sanitation systems, and so on; and to assist the public health agencies of member nations.

Apr. 8: With his 715th home run, Hank Aaron had broken the home-run record that had been held by Babe Ruth since 1935. Aaron finished his career with 755 home runs.

Apr. 9: The Marquis de Lafayette was awarded citizenship first by Maryland and then by several other states.

Apr. 10: Joseph Pulitzer became one of the most powerful and highly regarded journalists in the United States. His will provided for a series of awards to be given annually for outstanding public service in American journalism and letters. There are 8 prizes for journalism, 5 for literature, and since 1943, one for musical composition.

Apr. 11: It was part of his war message in which he asked Congress for "forcible intervention" against Spain to establish peace in Cuba. His request was granted on April 20. The Spanish-American War, which was over a few months later, began.

Apr. 13: President Franklin Delano Roosevelt had died on April 12. As FDR's vice-president, Truman would become President.

Apr. 14: He said, "The South is avenged."

Apr. 17: Possible answers are ace, age, ago, ale, arch, are, cage, cagey, cagy, car, care, cargo, cay, char, charge, chore, clay, clear, clog, cog, coo, cool, cooler, core, cry, each, ear, era, gale, galore, gay, gear, glare, glary, glory, goo, gooey, goal, gore, gory, gray, grey, hag, hale, hare, hay, heal, hear, her, hero, hoary, hog, hole, holy, lace, lacer, lacy, lag, large, lay, layer, leg, log, loge, logo, lore, lye, lyre, oar, ogre, oleo, ore, race, rag, rage, ray, reach, roe, role, yea, yeah, year, and yore. Accept other correct answers.

Apr. 18: The San Andreas Fault is a major fracture in the Earth's crust. It results from the abutment, or touching, of two major plates of the Earth's crust. It is movement along the fault that caused the earthquake.

Apr. 19: He said it to about 70 Minutemen during the Battle of Lexington. It began the American Revolution. "They" referred to the British.

Apr. 20: Hot Springs National Park is in central Arkansas. It has 47 thermal springs. There are several hydrotheropeutic institutions located there. The Physical Medicine Center is also there. Over a million gallons of water with an average temperature of 143°F (62°C) flow from the spring every day.

Apr. 23: Benjamin Franklin wrote in a 1789 letter, "...in this world nothing is certain but death and taxes."

Apr. 24: The Library of Congress was destroyed during the War of 1812 when British troops marched on Washington, D.C., and burned the Capitol.

Apr. 26: Audubon was an ornithologist and artist. He painted every known species of North American bird in the early 19th century. His paintings were published as *The Birds of America*. (A quatrain is a 4-lined poem.)

Apr. 26: A clerihew is a biographical, humorous quatrain. Usually the person is named in the first line of the poem.

Apr. 27: Facts may include some of the following: There are about 180 species. They are members of the family *Picidae* and the order *Piciformes*. They probe for insects in the tree bark. They chisel nest holes in dead wood. They occur worldwide, but they are most abundant in South America and Southeast Asia. A few temperate-zone species migrate. A few species include acorn woodpecker, great spotted woodpecker, and red-headed woodpecker.

Apr. 28: The Monroe Doctrine warned European nations not to intervene in the Western Hemisphere.

Apr. 29: "Onomatopoeia" is the formation or use of words that imitate what they denote. Some examples are *buzz, hiss, bang, whisper, moo, crash,* and *choochoo.*

Apr. 30: He was engineer on the Illinois Central locomotive, Number 382. The locomotive hit the caboose of a freight train that had been incompletely switched. Jones was the only one killed. His death at the throttle of the "Cannonball" led to his rise to national fame.

Optical Illusions (page 17)

The half of the ring on the white background appears darker because of contrast.

You see 6 cubes if you see the black diamonds as tops. You see 7 cubes if you see the black diamonds as bottoms.

International Children's Book Day (page 20)

Some of Andersen's tales are "The Tinderbox," "The Little Mermaid," "The Emperor's New Clothes," "The Snow Queen," "The Ugly Duckling," and "The Constant Tin Soldier."

Primates (pages 22–23)

1. Human	3. Monkey	5. Tarsier	7. Chimpanzee	9. Lemur	11. Marmoset
2. Baboon	4. Gorilla	6. Mandrill	8. Gibbon	10. Orangutan	

Modern humans belong to the species *homo sapiens*.

Chimpanzees live in the forests and swamps of tropical Africa. They spend time both in the trees and on the ground. They sleep in trees and build nests of branches and leaves. Chimps usually live in small groups.

Chimps are mainly vegetarian. Fruits, leaves, and seeds are an important part of their diet. Termites and ants are also included in their diet.

Koko is a Lowland gorilla who was taught American Sign Language by Dr. Francine Patterson.

Ms. Fossey, like Jane Goodall, lived in the wild in order to learn about the daily life of the great apes. Ms. Fossey was known for her work with mountain gorillas. She changed the stereotype of gorillas as stupid, aggressive animals. She alerted the world to the problem of poachers and was eventually killed because of her work.

Daylight Savings Time (page 24)

You lose an hour of sleep when you set the clock ahead if you have to get up at a certain time.

During the war they wanted to save fuel by lessening the need for artificial light in the evening.

Longitude and Time Zones (pages 25–26)

If it is midnight in New York, it is 11:00 P.M. in any city in the Central Time Zone.

The imaginary line called the International Date Line generally follows the 180th meridian. It runs through the middle of the Pacific Ocean where few people live and it zigzags around any land it meets. It is always one day later west of the line than east of the line; therefore, it would be January 4.

Chicago is in the Central Time Zone. Miami is in the Eastern Time Zone. Salt Lake City is in the Mountain Time Zone. Las Vegas is in the Pacific Time Zone.

The lines zigzag so that cities and towns aren't divided into two zones.

Booker T. Washington (pages 27–29)

The sentences should be rewritten in the following order: 6, 11, 4, 2, 7, 3, 5, 9, 10, 8, and 1.

What Does the "T" Stand For?

1. Tuskegee	3. Lincoln	5. Slave	7. Teacher	9. Trades
2. Alabama	4. Civil	6. Free	8. Normal	10. Coal

The "T" stands for Taliaferro.

Up From Slavery is an autobiography.

George Washington Carver was a great agricultural scientist. He had his laboratory at the Tuskegee Institute. Carver was a tremendous help in the revival of Southern farming. He is especially known for his studies of uses of the peanut. Carver and Washington became close friends.

W.E.B. Du Bois was the first black to earn a Ph.D. at Harvard University. He was a founder of the NAACP. Du Bois felt that Washington stressed manual labor rather than higher education. He also believed that Washington overlooked the discrimination and racial barriers that still existed.

The Space Shuttle (page 32)

The space shuttle lands like a glider.

It was different from previous spacecraft because it could go into space and come back again repeatedly.

Thomas Jefferson (pages 33–36)

Vocabulary Match-up

1. E	5. A	9. F	13. D	17. G
2. H	6. T	10. R	14. Q	18. M
3. K	7. C	11. I	15. J	19. L
4. N	8. S	12. B	16. O	20. P

Patrick Henry was the first governor of Virginia.

Thomas Jefferson and his followers became known as Democratic-Republicans. (Sometimes they were simply called Republicans.) They believed in states' rights and the strict interpretation of the Constitution. They believed the common people should be given more power in the government. Their support came from small farmers, frontier settlers, and northern laborers. Alexander Hamilton and his followers were known as Federalists. They favored a strong central government run by the rich. They also favored a national bank.

Until 1804 the person with the most votes became President; the runner-up became Vice-President. In 1804 the law was changed so that the President and Vice-President ran on the same ticket.

Pan-American Day (pages 37–38)

Cuba was expelled in 1962. The OAS wanted to isolate Fidel Castro's regime there. Cuba is an island republic in the Caribbean; it is south of Florida.

The Monroe Doctrine warned European nations against interfering in affairs of the governments of the Western Hemisphere. Especially important is the principle that an attack upon a member state would be considered an attack on all.

Name That Capital!

1. F	5. A	9. O	13. D	17. L
2. K	6. J	10. C	14. I	18. G
3. Q	7. H	11. N	15. T	19. P
4. B	8. M	12. S	16. E	20. R

An American Dictionary (pages 39–42)

The American Spelling Book, better known as the "Blue-Backed Speller," was first published in 1783. It provided the bulk of Webster's income for the rest of his life.

A dictionary is a reference work that provides spelling, meanings, pronunciation, and origins of words.

It's All in the Dictionary

1. not	3. ton	5. iron	7. rain	9. riot
2. city	4. rant	6. train	8. drain	10. yard

Rhyme-Time Definitions

1. a mad dad	3. a green queen	5. a lucky ducky	7. a quick chick	9. a wet pet	11. a fat rat
2. an ape cape	4. a certain curtain	6. a fake snake	8. a hoggy froggy	10. a yellow fellow	

The letters spell "April Shower."

Find It! (pages 44–47)
3. Martin Luther King, Jr., was assassinated on April 4, 1968.
5. The Battle of Shiloh took place on April 6 and 7, 1862.
7. General Lee surrendered to General Grant.
13. Wilbur and his brother Orville are known for the invention of the airplane.
15. Henry Wadsworth Longfellow wrote "Paul Revere's Ride."
16. Queen Isabella I of Castille sponsored the expeditions of Christopher Columbus.
19. Madeline is the main character in Ludwig Bemelmans famous children's books.

Holocaust Memorial Day (page 48)
Warsaw is in Poland.

Webster's Intermediate Dictionary defines "martyr" as "a person who suffers death rather than give up his or her religion" or "one who sacrifices life or something of great value for a principle or cause."

Ben and Me **(pages 49–59)**
Foreword and Chapter I: Vocabulary   1. k   2. e   3. h   4. a   5. f   6. b   7. i   8. c   9. j   10. d   11. g
Foreword and Chapter I: Comprehension and Discussion
    1. It belonged to a mouse.
    2. He, Amos the mouse, was responsible.
    3. They ate the prayer books and services.
    4. He hoped to find a way to help the others. At least it would be one less mouth to feed.
    5. He made his home in Benjamin Franklin's fur cap.
Foreword and Chapter I: Follow-up Activities
    2. Rodents have large incisors adapted for gnawing or nibbling. Rats, squirrels, chipmunks, groundhogs, and beavers are also rodents.
Chapters II and III: Vocabulary   1. f   2. i   3. a   4. c   5. k   6. d   7. h   8. b   9. l   10. e   11. j   12. g
Chapters II and III: Comprehension and Discussion
    1. Amos remembered the way his family gathered around the hot chestnut, which radiated heat and warmed the entire room.
    2. He suggested a layer of sand. He got the idea from the stories the shiprats told about how the sailors built their cooking fires aboard ship.
    3. Amos was hungry. Ben was so involved in the creation of the stove that he hadn't thought about food.
    4. He said, "We've done it!" recognizing Amos's contribution.
    5. Ben would provide a home, food, and clothing for Amos. He would also arrange for food to be delivered to Amos's family twice a week. In turn, Amos would aid and advise Ben in all matters.
Chapters IV and V: Vocabulary   1. d   2. i   3. k   4. l   5. f   6. a   7. g   8. b   9. c   10. h   11. e   12. j
Chapters IV and V: Comprehension and Discussion
    1. He scurried up a small sapling.
    2. He thought Amos was in it and probably feared for his life.
    3. A "yokel" is a naive or gullible country person. The two yokels found the pile of clothing and the watch with Benjamin Franklin's name engraved on it.
    4. He used the name Poor Richard.
    5. Amos had made changes in the Tide Table and in the risings and settings of the moon. A mob came after Ben for the problems these wrong predictions had caused. Ben convinced them that someone had perpetrated a hoax; however, he had figured out that Amos was responsible.
Chapters VI and VII: Vocabulary   1. d   2. g   3. j   4. l   5. i   6. a   7. c   8. e   9. h   10. k   11. b   12. f
Chapters VI and VII: Comprehension and Discussion
    1. Amos got a shock because static electricity was produced.
    2. It was called the Philosophical Society.
    3. They were gathered to witness Ben's exhibition of his achievements in working with electricity.
    4. Amos thought Ben had made mistakes when connecting the wires. The Governor received a strong electric shock. Ben thought it was a successful experiment because he learned the effects of strong electric shock on humans.
    5. Ben wanted to know if lightning was electrical.
Chapters VI and VII: Follow-up Activities
    1. Electricity flows more easily through some materials than others. Those materials that allow it to flow easily are called conductors. Those that do not allow electricity to flow through are called insulators. Metals are good conductors; so is water. Glass and other ceramics, wood, rubber, and many plastics are insulators. Amos was in a glass jar; the electricity couldn't flow through the glass.
    2. Sarcasm is a mocking remark, usually meant to ridicule. Amos said to Ben, "So you replaced them with a couple of pillows." He was taunting him for being so afraid.
Chapters VIII and IX: Vocabulary   1. f   2. d   3. h   4. j   5. l   6. a   7. k   8. b   9. c   10. e   11. g   12. i
Chapters VIII and IX: Comprehension and Discussion
    1. Amos and Ben had built a contraption in which Amos could slide up and down Ben's kite string. Ben had removed the car so that Amos would have to remain aloft during the storm.
    2. He agreed to stop experimenting with electricity.
    3. Ben was sent to England to present the colonists' grievances to the King and Parliament. Amos was going to go with him; however, he learned that Ben had convinced the captain to put up lightning rods.
    4. Red was Thomas Jefferson's mouse.
    5. It was based upon the "Manifesto," or list of grievances mice had suffered at the hands of Man. This document was drafted by Red. Amos gave it to Ben to read.
Chapters VIII and IX: Follow-up Activities
    1. Personification is the giving of human qualities to inanimate objects or ideas.
Chapters X and XI: Vocabulary   1. d   2. g   3. j   4. l   5. a   6. b   7. i   8. e   9. k   10. h   11. f   12. c
Chapters X and XI: Comprehension and Discussion
    1. The wheat grown at Mount Vernon was of excellent quality, and Amos always found some crumbs in his boot-tops and pocket flaps.
    2. He wanted Ben to appeal to France for monetary aid. The American soldiers were in desperate need of shoes, uniforms, powder, and arms.
    3. Yes, he succeeded in obtaining a loan of millions of francs.
    4. She had dozens of cats and a dog.

5. Sophia was a beautiful white mouse given refuge by Madame Brillon. Her husband was exiled to America, and her children were being held captive in Versailles. Amos promised not to rest until she, her husband, and her children were reunited in Philadelphia.

Chapters X and XI: Follow-up Activities
1. In Chapter X the author used the following words instead of *said: whispered, suggested, hissed, replied,* and *added.*
2. Simile is the comparison of two unlike things using the words *like* or *as.*

Chapters XII and XIII: Vocabulary   1. d   2. g   3. h   4. b   5. a   6. f   7. k   8. i   9. c   10. j   11.e

Chapters XII and XIII: Comprehension and Discussion
1. They received the news that Lord Cornwallis had surrendered and that the Colonies were free.
2. We often use the word *infested* if mice or other animals considered pests are in a place in large number.
3. They were enticed by the food that had been set out.
4. The sailor rats of John Paul Jones rescued them.
5. They blamed him for the wild confusion because the mice had come from him. "Ben fairly dripped mice!"

Chapters XII and XIII: Follow-up Activities
1. Von Steuben was a German officer who came to America in 1777. A master of precision drills, he was appointed to train the undisciplined Continental forces stationed at Valley Forge, PA. He is credited with drilling the men until they were able to respond to verbal commands.
2. The Marquis de Lafayette was a French noble who fought with the Americans against the British; he was appointed a major general and fought with distinction at the Battle of Brandywine, PA. He also helped the Colonists' cause by convincing Louis XVI of France to send men and ships to aid the Americans.

Chapters XIV and XVII: Vocabulary   1. b   2. e   3. g   4. i   5. k   6. l   7. h   8. a   9. j   10. c   11. f   12. d

Chapters XIV and XVII: Comprehension and Discussion
1. Amos convinced Ben that they would receive a hero's welcome in America.
2. He would give him a new fur cap for his birthday. This new cap had no place for Amos.
3. Amos's mother gave him one earmuff; she didn't have time to finish the other, but promised to complete it before the cold weather. His father gave him a watch charm, which he had gnawed from the shell of a black walnut.
4. Ben's old hat was very shabby and he was somewhat ashamed to wear it. He loved the new hat and thought it was magnificent. On the other hand, Ben worried because there was no place for Amos.
5. He told Ben that he would always be able to find him in his old fur cap hanging on his bedpost if he needed him. He warned him to watch out for mudholes (because he wouldn't be in his cap to guide him).

John Muir (pages 60–61)
Muir Woods is located in Marin County, California.

Buck Island Reef National Monument contains an underwater trail. Snorkelers explore the underwater trail through the tropical reef. Plaques along the way describe the fish and other sea life.

Our Environment (pages 63–71)
The Greenhouse Effect
Carbon dioxide allows the shorter, visible rays of the sun to pass through it and shine on the earth. These light rays are converted into heat energy. When the earth and the other heated surfaces on it re-radiate this heat energy, it is in the form of longer, invisible rays; these rays are called infrared rays. Although the carbon dioxide cannot absorb the shorter, visible rays, it can absorb the longer, invisible ones. The carbon dioxide, therefore, traps the heated rays. The more carbon dioxide in the atmosphere, the more heat energy that is trapped.

Silent Spring, published in 1962, was written to alert readers to the dangers of using pesticides such as DDT. She believed DDT was responsible for the destruction of many eagles by causing them to lay soft-shelled eggs.

Scrambled Animals of the Amazon
1. Amazon parrot	3. owl-faced monkey	5. puma	7. jaguar	9. tapir	11. two-toed sloth
2. scarlet macaw	4. boa constrictor	6. iguana	8. tree frog	10. hummingbird	12. snail

***The Lorax* (page 72)**
1. It is a story in rhyme.
2. The Once-ler narrates most of the book.
3. The Once-ler sold Thneeds.
4. The Once-ler wanted to use the soft tuft to knit a Thneed.
5. The Lorax popped out of the stump.
6. The trees needed protection and couldn't speak for themselves.
7. The Bar-ba-loots depended on the Truffula Fruits for their food. Because the trees were cut down, there was not enough food to go around. The Swomee-Swans left; they couldn't sing because of the smog the Once-ler's factory had created. The Humming-Fish left because the Once-ler had dumped the waste from his factory into the pond where they swam; the pond was too polluted for the fish to live in it.
9. Charts should include the following information: The **roots** grow in the ground and usually spread about as wide as the **branches.** The stem is called a **trunk.** The outside of the trunk is called the **bark.** Students may also include the **cambium,** which is just inside the bark where the new wood is growing; the **sapwood,** which is the next layer in; and the **heartwood,** which is the hard dead core at the center.
10. Before the Once-ler arrived, the Truffula Trees were plentiful. The air and water were clean. Many different creatures inhabited the land. After the Once-ler was there a while, the trees were gone, smog filled the air, and the pond was polluted. Only the Once-ler remained. All the other creatures were forced to move away. Very little remained the same; however, at the end we see the potential for things to return to the way they once were.
11. The Once-ler was out of business because he had cut down all the trees, which were the source of the raw material he needed for his Thneeds. Perhaps he could have found a way to harvest the tufts without cutting down the trees.
12. Answers will vary, but the following facts may be included: Trees take in carbon dioxide and give off oxygen, thereby helping to keep down the level of carbon dioxide in our atmosphere. They provide lumber, fruit, nuts, and paper products. They beautify the land and provide shade. They provide homes for animals.

Math Fun (pages 73–75)
SITUATION NO. 1: If all six sit up front, the tickets will cost $140.00. If the mother and father sit in the main section and the others sit up front, the cost will be $126.00. If they all sit in the balcony instead of all sitting up front, they will save $66.00.

SITUATION NO. 2: In addition to the soda and hot dog, you can buy cotton candy and will have 15 cents left. It would cost $12.50 to buy one of everything. Scott has enough; he would have 15 cents left over. You would have to borrow $2.35 to buy those things.

SITUATION NO. 3: There are 24 pieces. If shared equally, each would have four pieces. If one friend has 1 piece and another has 3 pieces, each of the others can have 5 pieces. Friend No. 1 will pay $2.50; Friend No. 2 will pay $3.75; Friend No. 3 will pay $6.25; Friend No. 4 will pay $7.50; Friend No. 5 will pay $5.00; and Friend No. 6 will pay $5.00. The total bill is $30.00. EXTRA: Friend No. 1 will leave 38 cents; Friend No. 2 will leave 56 cents; Friend No. 3 will leave 94 cents; Friend No. 4 will leave $1.13; Friend No. 5 will leave 75 cents; and Friend No. 6 will leave 75 cents. The total tip is $4.51.

(Elicit from the students why there is an extra penny.)

Spring Garden (pages 76–79)
Wind helps spread pollen. So do birds, bees, and other insects.

Wanderers of the Sky: Birds (pages 80–82)
Syllogisms
1. Therefore, the robin is a bird.
2. Therefore, the parrot is warm-blooded.
3. Therefore, the mockingbird belongs to the class *Aves*.
4. Invalid: The major premise does not say "only." According to the statement, therefore, other animals can also have backbones.
5. Invalid: The major premise says "most," not "all." According to the statement, therefore, some birds can care for themselves.
6. Invalid: The major premise does not say "only." According to the statement, other animals can also give birth to their young by laying eggs.

Bird Crossword:

A War on Polio (page 83)
Dr. Sabin's vaccine was administered orally.

Words include elm, emit, empty, ill, isle, its, lest, let, lie, lime, lip, lisp, list, lit, loom, loop, loose, lop, lope, lore, lose, lost, lot, lye, melt, mile, mill, mist, mite, mole, molt, moo, moose, mop, mope, most, oil, oily, omit, oops, pelt, pest, pet, pie, pile, pill, plot, ploy, ply, poem, poet, pole, polio, pool, post, pot, sell, set, sill, silt, sit, site, slim, slime, slip, slit, slop, slope, slot, sly, soil, sop, spell, spill, spilt, split, spool, spot, spy, stem, step, stile, still, stole, stop, sty, style, tell, tie, tile, till, time, toe, toil, too, tool, top, toy, yell, yes, and yet. Accept other appropriate answers.

Passover (pages 85–86)
1. P   2. E   3. S   4. A   5. C   6. H   Another name for Passover is *Pesach*.
Reclining at the table was once a sign of a free man. Reclining is a reminder that the Jews were once slaves, but that now they are free.

Arbor Day (page 87)
To be a tree, a plant must be perennial; in other words, it must renew its growth each year. It must have a single, self-supporting trunk with woody tissues. Most trees also have secondary limbs, called branches.
Evergreens retain their foliage throughout the year. Deciduous trees lose their leaves during part of the year. Sometimes whether a tree is evergreen or deciduous depends on the climate. Some trees are evergreen in tropical regions that are always humid but deciduous in areas where wet and dry seasons alternate.

The Giving Tree (page 88)
1. It was an apple tree.
2. He made them into a crown and played king of the forest.
3. He swung from the branches.
4. The tree offered to give him its apples to sell.
5. The tree offered to give him its branches to build a house.
6. The tree offered to give him its trunk to build a boat.
12. A parasite is an organism that grows, feeds, and lives on or in another organism; it does not contribute to that organism's survival. A parasitic relationship is one that relates to or is characteristic of a parasite. A symbiotic relationship, on the other hand, is one of mutual benefit or dependence.

111

National Wildlife Week Word Search (page 89)

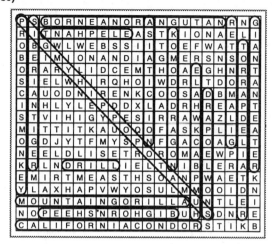

Maryland (page 91)

1. B   2. A   3. L   4. T   5. I   6. M   7. O   8. R   9. E

Louisiana (page 92)

The name of the state song is "You Are My Sunshine."

Spring Sports Logic (page 97)

1. racket   2. tennis   3. soccer   4. golf ball   5. team   (Accept other appropriate answers.)
6. racket (others are golf terms)   7. putt (others are tennis terms)   8. birdie (others are soccer terms)
9. offside (others are baseball terms)   10. tobogganing (others are warm-weather sports)

A Different Kind of Puzzle (page 98)

1. Falling in love
2. Head over heels in love
3. Singing in the rain
4. Rose in bloom
5. Long underwear
6. Run around the bases
7. Hole-in-one
8. Man overboard!

April Crossword (page 100)

112